SYLVIE GIRARD-LAGORCE

The Book of

ROSES

PHOTOGRAPHS
BY CHRISTIAN SARRAMON

STYLIST NELLO RENAULT

Flammarion

This bouquet of roses
is for
Suzanne Girard

Editorial direction: Ghislaine Bavoillot
Editorial management: Sophy Thompson
Translated from the French by
Josephine Bacon, American Eyes Ltd.
Copy-editing: Bernard Wooding
Additional research by Suzanne Pickford
Color separation: Sele Offset, Italy

ISBN: 2-080-10539-6
Numéro d'édition: FA0539-XII-00
Dépôt légal: décembre 2000
Printed in Spain

Contents

Once Upon a Time There Was a Rose

O my Luve's like a red, red rose,
That's newly sprung in June;
O my Luve's like the melodie
That's sweetly play'd in tune.

As fair art thou, my bonnie lass,
So deep in luve am I;
And I will luve thee still, my Dear,
Till a' the seas gang dry...

Robert Burns, A Red, Red Rose

Seductive yet subtle, these "Roses
on a White Background" (1823)
by the French painter Antoine Berjon
are of an exquisite simplicity (page 8),
whereas the "Study of Roses" (1909)
by Adolphe Castex-Degrange
(facing page), another French painter,
evokes the moving fragility of the flower.
Both painters are from the Lyons school,
famous for its flower paintings.

In the words of Edna St. Vincent Millay, "Beauty never slumbers; / All is in her name; / But the rose remembers / The dust from which it came." When admiring these full-blown, fragrant, dew-laden blooms in all their luscious and voluptuous glory, one can only marvel at the myths and legends behind the luminous and sensual palette of their many colors and their mystery.

The white rose is said to have arisen from sea foam or from the drops of sweat of the Prophet Mohammed, and the red rose is said to be tinted by the blood of Aphrodite, who was wounded by the thorns that separated her from the fair Adonis. In the Orient, the red rose is supposed to have been born from a voluptuous smile. The Christian mystics saw it blossom on the tortured body of Christ, while in India, a nightingale that wanted to delight men with its nocturnal singing, pressed itself against the thorns of a snow-white rose tree in order to stay awake. The rose has always possessed a unique magic. "Sing of them, my heart, those gardens that are unknown to you," wrote the German poet Rainer Maria Rilke. "The water and the roses of Isfahan or of Shiraz, sing of them, oh happiness, celebrate them as incomparable...."

A Flower Rich in Symbolism

Of all the wild flowers, and all the flower cultivated since Antiquity in China, Greece, and the Orient, it is the rose that has the richest symbolism. The white rose represents purity and innocence, the red—passion and bloodshed, sensuality as well as martyrdom. The tiny bud with its tightly furled petals soon opens out into the velvety, languid richness of the full-blown flower, an allegory for the passage from innocence to maturity. The velvety softness of the thick petals conceals the sharp pain of the piercing thorns. Love and suffering, in the same dizzying beauty. The rose has always held pride of place among the flowers of the world. Through rites, through beliefs, through custom or by its simple emotive power,

White or red, the rose speaks of innocence and purity, of flame and passion. These are the original colors of the queen of flowers, which, according to an ancient legend, was born from sea foam.

It is no accident that the cabbage rose has been dubbed "the painter's rose." It has been the subject of numerous paintings since the days of the Dutch masters. It is the romantic rose par excellence, gracefully bowing its head under the weight of its innumerable petals, as in the painting below, entitled "Rose Bush" (1871) by Jean-Pierre Laÿs. Since the High Middle Ages, the rose has been associated with the Virgin Mary, combining her purity with the shedding of Christ's blood. Saint-Jean Simon (180-1860) produced this typical, nineteenth-century neo-Gothic painting (facing page) entitled "Virgin in a Rose Bush."

for more than two thousand years the rose has been linked with childbirth, virginity, the loss of virginity, carnal pleasures, the ephemeral nature of the human body, the death of the body, and concepts of regeneration and spiritual renaissance. Saint Ambrose made this comparison clear when he clamied that of all the flowers, the rose is the only one to come from Paradise. But in the Garden of Eden, it had no thorns. When it dropped to earth after the Fall, it armed itself with spikes, yet it retained its moving beauty and divine fragrance, as a sign to the human race that there is hope of salvation. When Antoine de Saint-Exupéry's Little Prince defended the roses who were accused of having thorns "out of pure malice," he exclaimed, "flowers are weak, they are naive. They comfort themselves as best they can. They think themselves very dangerous with their thorns…."

Dante, guided by Beatrice, has a dazzling vision of the Mystic Rose in the last lines of his *Divine Comedy*. It is the white rose, *Rosa candida*, the symbol of pure, divine love. "Here is the rose in which the Word is made Flesh," he wrote. This is the rose which is reproduced in stone in the Gothic cathedrals, in the rose windows, those huge wheels of stone and stained glass (the rose window of Notre-Dame in Paris is 13 meters [43 feet] in diameter), stylizations of the flower that represents the soul of the world, and which is also a symbol of the Virgin Mary, mother of Jesus Christ, one of whose titles is "the Mystical Rose." A crown of white roses became her symbol, but it has also been attributed to the mystical saints, among them Saint Dorothea, who carries roses in a basket, Saint Casilda, Saint Elizabeth of Portugal, and Saint Rose of Viterbo. It is the symbol of postulants taking the veil. The allegorical garden described in the Song of Songs, the walled garden in which the most beautiful flowers grew, was replaced in the Middle Ages by the metaphor of the Church over which the Virgin Mary presided in all her glory, ruling the garden of innocence, in which the rose, first among flowers, is the very embodiment of virtue. According to legend, Saint Dominic received as a gift from the Virgin Mary a rose that had blossomed on the crown of thorns worn by Christ.

At her request, he picked a bouquet of roses with which to recite the first rosary. Subsequently, rosaries were made of beads formed from roses that were dried, crushed, and perfumed with attar of roses.

The *Roman de la Rose,* written by Guillaume de Lorris and Jean de Meung in the latter half of the thirteenth century—and translated from French by Geoffrey Chaucer as *The Romaunt of the Rose*—is one of the most famous poems of courtly love. Set in the Garden of Delights, it recounts the quest of the lover who endures every peril to attain his ultimate goal: to pick the rose and caress its petals, open the flower, and bury himself in it (symbolic of the deflowering his virgin bride). When Sleeping Beauty, piously guarded by the impenetrable hedge of thorns, is awakened with a kiss by Prince Charming, in the ultimate romance on the same theme, life reawakens in the enchanted castle. The hymen has been broken, they will have many children… Even today, a gift of red roses is still the surest way of declaring undying love. Among the Gypsies, after a wedding, a reddened handkerchief folded into the shape of a rose is shown to the guests.

Roman and Persian Roses

The voluptuousness of the rose caused it to be dedicated to love, first by the Greeks and then by the Romans. The velvety petals of the flower made it a natural adjunct to celebrations and banquets. A strongly scented rose, probably the damask rose, still cultivated in France, Turkey, Bulgaria, and Morocco for its exquisite perfume, was grown in southern Italy. These were the roses showered upon the guests at their infamous orgies.

Wearing wreaths of roses on their heads and round their necks (the scent of the rose was reputed to have the magic power of curing a hangover), wealthy patricians reclined on beds of roses, drinking from cups in which petals floated. The feast of Rosalia, in May, was celebrated by placing cut roses on the tombs of ancestors and distributing the *lares* and *penates,* as the rose-flavored offerings were known. It was the

The decadence of the Roman Empire was the inspiration for the extravagant vision of the Victorian painter, Lawrence Alma-Tadema, entitled "The Roses of Heliogabalus." It was inspired by a true story in the life of the young Roman emperor who was obsessed with luxury and pleasure (facing page and below). In ancient times, a wreath of roses was a mark of divine favor. This tradition persisted until the Christian era (bottom, detail of a painting by Edward Burne-Jones, "Pilgrim at the Gate of Idleness," 1874).

Roses were celebrated with lyricism by the authors of antiquity, and they have always been an inspiration for art (above, "Summer" by W.E. Reynold, 1862). The rose is indeed the loveliest of flowers (below, "Charles de Gaulle," a rose by Meilland, which, like "Mamy Blue," is one of the few "blue" roses).

Emperor Nero who launched the fashion for showers of roses during his banquets, but this delightful whim turned into a nightmare when the Emperor Heliogabalus took it too far. He replaced the few armfuls of roses sprinkled lightly over the guests by huge masses of blooms which were heaped over those present, literally suffocating them.

But the Romans' excessive love of roses contained the portents of disaster. The flower of life and love, of exquisite beauty to delight the soul and the eyes, has a very short life, making it the representative of death and decrepitude, the ever-present reminder of the fragility of existence: the life of a rose is the space of a morning. Hecate, the Greek goddess of the underworld with her dogs of death, who comes to seek out the souls of the departed, wears a crown of five-petaled roses.

The gardens of ancient Persia abounded with flowers of all kinds, but especially with roses. They were places of rest and meditation, "far from the madding crowd," which inspired the Persian poets and their masterpieces of mosaic and embroidery, magnificently woven carpets, and sumptuous jewels. In the thirteenth century, the poet Saadi wrote *The Garden of Roses*, an erotic and mystic moral treatise which became famous well beyond the borders of Islam. Saadi made the rose garden the epitome of ecstasy, and the rose the absolute model of correct behavior. One reads in it, for example, that any plant that grows near a rosebush takes on its fragrance, as a parable on the theme of "tell me who your friends are and I will tell you what you are...." Omar Khayyam, another Persian poet and mathematician who lived in the ninth century B.C.E., was anguished by the shortness of life. In his famous *Rubaiyat* quatrains, he talks of women, roses, and wine in a single celebration of life: "Morning a thousand Roses brings, you say; Yes, but where lives the Rose of Yesterday?"

Alchemy and Secrecy

The rose in East and West has gathered even more symbolism and significance down the ages than the lotus of the Far East. The red rose is the sign of loss of virginity, of the unleashing of the passions of the flesh; in the vocabulary of allegory it becomes the emblem of revolution, the red rose brandished by those fighting for a just cause. Red is also the color of the rose venerated by the esoteric sect known as the Rosicrucians. Among the flowers in the alchemist's garden, the white rose was associated with the "small work," the transmutation of base metals into silver, while the red rose meant the transmutation of base metals into gold, known as the "great work."

This spiritual concordance has inspired the creation of the garden at Eygalières, in Provence, which was imagined as an initiatory circuit by the landscape gardeners Arnaud Maurières and Eric Ossart. They have produced many visual and olfactory impressions to gorge the senses, ending with the walled garden known as "the work in red," in which thirty red rosebushes flourish in a riot of color. According to legend, Venus wanted to keep her love life

According to a tradition that dates back to the eleventh century, on the fourth Sunday in Lent, the pope blessed a golden rose, symbolizing the resurrection, and awarded it to a prominent personage. This example, which can be seen at Andechs in Germany, is probably the work of a Florentine goldsmith who was active in Rome about 1450.

Ever since the medieval allegory entitled "Le Roman de la Rose," the rose has been the eternal symbol of womanhood, flourishing in a walled garden, the ideal woman whom the knight in shining armor passionately desires to pluck and keep for himself. Poets and artists have used the rose as the symbol of courtly love. The symbol was a favorite with the Pre-Raphaelite movement in nineteenth-century England, which took its inspiration from the paintings of the Italian old masters (above, "The Heart of the Rose" by Edward Burne-Jones). The red rose is also the symbol of England, as worn on a white strip by England's national rugby team (below).

secret, so she gave a rose, her emblem, to the god of Silence, Harpocrates. The Romans perpetuated the myth by suspending a rose from the ceiling of a room to guarantee the discretion concerning whatever was uttered there. Even today, the expression *sub rosa* ("under the rose") is used in both German and English to mean, "in the strictest confidence."

Roses as Political Symbols

The rose of York is red just as the rose of Lancaster is white. The rose may be pleasing to poets and lovers but it also rules over one of the blackest periods of the history of England, the Wars of the Roses, a conflict which Shakespeare summarizes as follows in *Henry VI*, *Part II*: "And here I prophesy: this brawl to-day, grown to this faction in the Temple-garden, shall send between the red rose and the white, a thousand souls to death and deadly night." The men of Lancaster took the red rose as their emblem, while the House of York chose the white rose. The symbolism of the Tudor rose, with its two rows of five petals, one white, one red, was the reconciliation of both parties in a single royal house, thirty years after the Wars of the Roses had ended. The Tudor rose is still a royal symbol, and a red rose is embroidered on the shirts of the English rugby team.

There is nothing modern about the use of the rose as a warrior's emblem. Homer wrote that roses featured in the designs on both Hector's helmet and Achilles' shield. Throughout history, men and women, orders and political parties, associations and coats of arms, have been sculpted, chiseled, engraved, and painted with rose motifs. George Herbert (1593–1633), the English poet priest, wrote in his poem *The Rose*:

What is fairer than a rose?
What is sweeter? Yet it purgeth,
Purgings enmitie disclose,
Enmitie forebearance urgeth.

The rose is also an ancient symbol of festivals and the commemoration of historic events. Every year, on June 24, the representatives of one of the oldest religious foundations in London offer the Lord Mayor a red rose on a cushion, in payment of a tax originally owed by a certain Robert Knollys. He was ordered to pay this tax *ad vitam eternam* (for all eternity) in the fourteenth century, for the crime of having created a passage between two houses that he owned on either side of Seething Lane, without first asking permission from the Court of Common Council. At the other end of Europe, the Catalans celebrate Saint George's Day, April 23, by giving each other a rose and a book.

A fitting tribute in a country whose first president was a rose grower, the rose was named America's national floral emblem in 1986, and is also the state flower in Georgia, Iowa, New York, North Dakota, and the District of Columbia.

For days and days
I see that you hesitate
In your tightly restrictive corset.
Rose which, in being born, is an imitation
Of the slow onset of death in reverse.
Does your innumerable state let you know
In a mixture in which everything is confused,
That ineffable accord of nothingness and being
Of which we are unaware?
Rainer Maria Rilke, "The Rose that Came Very Late."

The Rose and Poetry

Nicholas Culpeper, the great herbalist, wrote in *An English Herbal Enlarged*, "What a pother have authors made with Roses! What a racket they have kept!"

As the subject of all these myths, as the sometimes banal vehicle for innumerable messages from god and from man, messages of love and death, symbol of the Christian heaven and the Persian paradise—"grandiose, divine, heady flower of the fawn and of the Christian virgin," in the words of Federico García Lorca—the rose is the eternal symbol of perfection. Are not its petals multiples of five? Five or ten in the single rose, ten, fifteen, and more in the double rose. Five, a perfect number, a sign of union, harmony, and balance. And yet, how enigmatic is the rose!

"Rose, oh pure contradiction," wrote Rainer Maria Rilke (who, according to a story that is too romantic to be true, is said to have died from the prick of a rose thorn), "the voluptuousness of being the sleep of no one under so many eyelids."

Roses in the Garden

The villa overhung the slope of its hill and the long valley of the Arno, hazy with Italian color. It had a narrow garden, in the manner of a terrace, productive chiefly of tangles of wild roses and old stone benches, mossy and sun-warmed...

Henry James, The Portrait of a Lady

Despite their apparent fragility, roses are actually quite hardy plants whose exceptional longevity enables them to retain their beauty season after season (right). Roses that are pale in color are always shown to their best advantage against a contrasting dark green background. A bench on a lawn, between shadow and sunlight, where the petals fall in cascades, is the perfect place for idyllic repose (facing page).

The bulky rose-growers' catalogues that drop onto the mat with a thud, their numerous pages a riot of color, contain hundreds and hundreds of rose names. The world of roses sometimes seems to be overcrowded. It appears to be almost impossible to find one's way around the long scientific names and the long-winded or over-imaginative "common" names. This view was shared by the writer, Colette: "What do I need with your official nomenclature, littered with the names of retired generals, retired industrialists and other bigwigs?" she wrote in *Prisons and Paradise*. "In President Herriot's case I'll let it pass because he was an enthusiastic and skilled gardener. But in my religion I have a better name for you, Rose. In secret, I call you Purple Peach, Apricot Liqueur, Snow, Fairy, Black Beauty, you who gloriously pays homage to a truly pagan name—Cuisse de Nymphe Emue [thigh of the blushing nymph]!"

The true lover of gardens, guided by fragrances and colors, forms and volumes, resorts to his or her own thoughts and memories. The French couturier, Jean-Charles de Castelbajac, remembers his first garden: "It was the school kitchen garden. Today, I have made my dream come true at my home in Gers. I have planted trees and a thousand rosebushes. I have pompom roses and modern roses such as 'Gina Lollobrigida' in every hue. The idea of creating this rose garden, which is planted over an old cemetery, simply came to me as an inspiration. In June, it is magnificent!"

Rose Gardens

From the emergence of the first bud to the shedding of the petals, a rose is never the same. It changes depending on its position in the garden, the amount of exposure it gets, the time of year, the time of day, whether there is a fine mist of rain or bright sunshine. A rose expresses itself differently in response to all these factors and this accounts for much of the

The Bagatelle Rose Garden in the Bois de Boulogne, Paris, holds an international competition annually for new rose varieties. Several thousand rosebushes are on show for visitors to inspect in several hundred different forms. There are double-petaled blooms (below) or single-petaled ones like "Patricia" (bottom). "Pink Cloud," on the facing page, lives up to its name. In 1899 at L'Haÿ, in the Val-de-Marne department of France, a garden was opened in which roses were the only plant. This was the first rose garden conservatory in the world (overleaf).

fascination it exerts. Each time roses bloom, you fall in love with them all over again. Enthusiasts would have you believe that planting a rose garden is always something of a love affair. There is the enchantment of "Belle de Crécy" nestling in greenery, its purplish buds turning almost mauve in bright sunlight, and the spectacular glory and old-fashioned beauty of "Honorine de Brabant" whose variegated blooms appear in late spring.

"Thérèse Bugnet," a tall rose tree with fuchsia-colored blooms, can be seen from afar and the lovely moss rose called "Salet" sprinkles the lawn with its faded pink petals. For the entrance to an orchard, a good choice would be "Martin des Senteurs," whose fragrance is reminiscent of a basket of tropical fruits, and the best rose to grow beneath bedroom windows is the aptly named "Belle Sultane," a sensual, velvety bloom with soft, floppy, velvety petals the color of pomegranates.

"Mermaid" is a climbing briar rose or eglantine, whose huge flowers are pale golden. It prefers warm, sunny walls. "Neige d'Avril" (April snow) cascades immaculately down a wall in early spring, as the name implies, as long as the weather is mild. "Omar Khayyam" is a rose whose seed was found on the poet's tomb in northern Iran. The flower it produces is shocking pink, and in bright sunlight it has the wonderful fragrance of the damask rose.

Modern roses have wonderful color and fragrance, and flower almost throughout the year, thus meeting every possible requirement. Climbing roses, stem roses, rosebushes, or rose trees, "weeping" or carpeting the ground, massive banks or miniatures, offer the greatest diversity for the purpose of covering a flowerbed or invading every corner of the garden. A climbing rose, such as the lovely ocher-yellow "Crépuscule" (dusk), will embellish the walls of a house, climb over a simple metal arch or cover a bower, border a garden path, or even entwine itself among the branches of an old fruit tree. Buried under the perfumed cascades of "New Dawn," even a simple garden shed will look like a fairytale castle. This rosebush, which smells of ripe fruits, is one of the

This climbing rose, known as "Cécile Brunner," climbs up an old barn in a park in Courson, France (facing page). Another good climber to train over a wall is "Alister Stella Gray," one of the favorite roses of the wine writer Hugh Johnson. Its small scented blooms last until December in a temperate climate.

Gertrude Jekyll, the English landscape gardener, created a wonderful rose garden at the house known as Bois des Moutiers at Varengeville-sur-Mer, in northern France. It consists of a succession of enclosures, "designed gardens" (above and top). In the "white garden," the paved avenue leading toward the house is bordered by banks of "Snow Fairy" rosebushes.

All rosebushes love the sun and these "Pierre de Ronsard" adore the weather of Provence. Here, they adorn a walled garden, the delightful open-air dining room of the Mas de Tourteron, a farmhouse in Gordes (below). In Giverny, the rose-covered tunnels produce a lovely color harmony and balance of shapes (bottom). The massed banks of blooms produced by "Centenaire de Lourdes" produce large bunches of a delicate rose whose color darkens in the fall. This classic French rose, created by Delbard, has been given the rather prosaic English name of "Mrs Jones."

favorites of Elizabeth, the Queen Mother, whose love of roses is reflected in the decoration of all her residences. "Albertine" is another of her favorites, with the salmon-pink buds and the coppery tones of its full-blown petals. "The dear old Albertine is resistant to almost everything," she once confided. She also loves the richly colored floribunda "Glenfiddich," named for the famous brand of Scotch whisky.

In Monet's garden at Giverny, with its riot of colors and shapes, a tapestry of a thousand flowers, it is still possible to distinguish the beauty of individual roses, such as "Madame Caroline Testout," named for a famous nineteenth-century fashion designer. It is full, heavy, and round, and an incredible satiny pink in color. The best roses in the village are to be found, however, in the garden of the Hôtel Baudy, frequented by the painter and his friends. A massed border of roses sweeps along the edges of the winding paths. This old-fashioned country garden is a little corner of romance, invaded by wild roses which look as if they have been plucked straight from a nineteenth-century still-life painting.

The rose-lover is deeply attached to his or her blooms and watches over their growth like an anxious parent. He or she tends them, encourages them, and gives them "good grades." This type of behavior was described by Marcel Proust when he wrote about his grandmother in *Swann's Way*, explaining how she would surreptitiously uproot the rose-tree stakes "so as to give the roses something of their naturalness, like a mother who runs her fingers through her son's hair to fluff up his flattened locks." This same affection is shared by Elizabeth von Arnim, in the story of her life in Germany, *Elizabeth and Her German Garden* (1898). "As a rule, my roses behaved exactly as I had hoped. The 'Viscountess Folkestone' and 'Laurette Messimy' were even magnificent. There is nothing more exquisite in the whole garden than these roses, with their tangled, coral-colored petals that lighten at the base to pale yellow."

To begin with, the rose only existed in its wild state. The various successive changes it has undergone are due

to factors that were originally a complete mystery, but were later mastered by man. Nowadays, there are literally thousands of roses that have been created by rose growers, so many that these hybrids have become very difficult to identify. That is why rosebushes, whether old or new varieties, are usually classified for convenience according to their height and purpose.

Every type of decor, every usage, and every composition is possible. There is the nonchalant flowering of a pink rose on the corner of a wall framed by ancient linden trees, or the naive charm of tiny rose trees towering over the vegetables of a kitchen garden, an ancient French custom. At the château of Saint-Jean-de-Beauregard, in the French department of Essonne, the marriage of vegetables, fruits, and flowers reaches the height of elegance, a superb color scheme in which roses and peonies predominate. "The rosebush is also the closest companion to the vine," declares André Ève, one of France's leading rose growers, whose garden at Pithiviers-le-Vieil in the Loiret department is open to the public and is a unique spectacle. "That is why I dedicated

At the priory of Notre-Dame d'Orsan, the climbing roses are like fragrant walls (facing page). Rosebushes are traditionally planted beside rows of grape vines to act as an indicator of mildew (below, an orchard in Provence). At the château of Saint-Jean-de-Beauregard, the kitchen garden is a brilliantly successful combination of fruits, vegetables, and flowers (bottom).

Louis Benech is another talented French landscapist who loves opulent blooms such as "Madame Isaac Pereire" (below), and the delicacy of hybrid tea rose (above). In the garden of the priory of Saint-Michel which he created, water, land, and sky form a bright and peaceful harmony (facing page). The masses of color created by the rosebushes are carefully integrated among the shrubbery (overleaf).

the rose I call 'Graves de Vayres,' created in 1999, to one of the best vineyards in Bordeaux. The rose is large and of that same deep, warm wine-red as a delicious Graves wine, flowing into your glass." When asked to name his favorite rose, "Mr. Old-fashioned Roses" hesitates for quite a long time, finally responding, "Perhaps it is 'Ghislaine de Féligonde,' whose ivory yellow glow brightens dark corners."

Some old-fashioned rose gardens seem to have emerged straight from a medieval bower of the type described by Boccaccio as the "garden of abundance" in *The Decameron*: "As for the edges of the paths, they were entirely hidden by the white and vermilion rosebushes. In the morning, and even toward midday, one could roam everywhere with delight in their fragrant shade, without ever being touched by the sun's rays." It is this magical atmosphere that the gardens of the priory of Notre-Dame d'Orsan purvey, where the cascades of pale roses seem to whisper secrets among the bowers and wooden arches, while a whole wall is covered with "Pierre de Ronsard" rambling roses. "The rose garden at Orsan, a mixture of pink and white, is of purely medieval inspiration, and it is the religious symbol *par excellence*, for it evokes the Virgin Mary," explains Sonia Lesot in the book she has written about these gardens. "It consists of two areas, which are like two small rooms for contemplation, carpeted with lawns…. From June onward, one walks beneath tunnels in the shade of climbing roses silhouetted against the brilliant blue background of the sky. Where the corridors meet, an arbor reaches up to the sky."

Climbing roses like to extend outward as well as upward. A magnificent pink climbing rose covers the red-brick façade of Sissinghurst Castle in Kent, from the bay window to the roof tiles. This was the home of Vita Sackville-West, who was "drunk on roses," in her own words. "I should like to know," she wrote, "the true identity of this 'Madame Lauriol du Barny' who gave her name to such a sumptuous flower. I assume she must have belonged to the *haute cocotterie* of Paris, or perhaps I am completely wrong and she was a perfectly respectable

The Roseraie de Berty near Largentière is a magnificent sight in June, when the rambling and climbing roses covering the tunnels and the trees are in full bloom (below, top and bottom).

woman, the wife of a rose-grower from Lyons...." There are fragrant rosebushes near shady resting places or monochrome red blooms covering the cracks in an old wall, a spectacular weeping rosebush serving as a focal point beside a smooth lawn or a carpet of roses creeping right up to the threshold of the house. Whether opulent or discreet, sophisticated or humble, half-hidden or fully exposed, brazen or discreet, roses are everywhere at Sissinghurst, where they can be seen to their best advantage in June and July.

How can one define the ineffable attraction of the rose in a garden, however modest? The rose plays every kind of role, it surprises, it shelters, it is a feast for the eyes. It is a subject for meditation and speaks to all of the senses. "Planting old-fashioned roses in one's garden is to travel back in time, to attempt to make time stand still for one's own pleasure, and slowly, imperceptibly, create a world in which each of us would like to live," explains Éléonore Cruse, owner of the Roseraie de Berty, a little floral paradise nestling in a remote valley among the forests of the Ardèche, in central France. Here hundreds of rosebushes produce masses of exuberant blooms. There are rambling and climbing roses trained over trees or arbors, creating an unforgettable sight. "Admire 'Paul Transon,'" recommends Cruse, "on the arch from which it cascades. It is one of the loveliest of the copper-tinted roses, with the fresh perfume of green apples. Or there is the spectacular 'Raubritter,' growing beside the pond, that extends its supple branches weighed down with round roses toward the motionless waterlilies."

Roses for the Four Seasons

From April through Christmas, a succession of delightfully colored roses brighten our gardens. "It is a delight that lasts for many long months," explains the fashion designer, Lolita Lempicka, admiringly. Her love for the garden came with that of her house which she bought about fifteen years ago.

"My rosebushes were collected on walks or on trips, and climb over the arches of a tunnel, exploding into a myriad of flowers in various hues of white, pink, or red." Certain rosebushes only flower once a year, with surprising vigor, but only for a short time. Others bloom in successive waves, while some remain in bloom almost continually, for as long as the weather is clement. Still others revive in the fall, coming into even more beautiful bloom than they did in May or June.

At the very outset of spring, there is the acidic freshness of the scent of "Neige d'Avril." This avalanche of graceful roses is a reminder of the immaculate whiteness of the last snows of winter. In southern Europe, April is also the month in which the "Canary Bird" blooms. The bright yellow blossoms of this compact bush are a brilliant foil to the blue clumps of forget-me-nots that also flower

"Pierre de Ronsard," a French variety named for the famous poet, is an old-fashioned rose in a delicate shade of pink, a hardy climbing plant, developed by Meilland Richardier. It flowers abundantly throughout the year (below), as if to echo Ronsard's own advice: "Believe me, thou shouldst live, wait not for the morrow, / But pluck the roses of life today...." In a magnificent array of immaculately white roses, the garden bower of Lolita Lempicka seems to have been conjured up by the designer herself to emulate the delicate white silk roses that blossom on the wedding dresses she creates (overleaf).

In Claude Pigeart's kitchen garden, at Wy-dit-Joli-Village, clouds of crimson lake "Mozart" eglantines with a white heart flower from June through the fall (above top). The carmine deepens with the heat, then turns pale again as flowering ends. "Lordly Oberon" (above) has round double flowers. It is pale pink and has a most delicious fragrance.

at this season. The large white blooms of "Nevada" open in mid-May as if singing a hymn to the first warm days, followed by the flowering of the magnificent "Madame Edouard Herriot," a coral-pink rose of infinite sweetness whose shades of ocher and terra are redolent of the warmth of summer.

Of course, the real rose season begins in June. The pale, downy white petals of "Madame Plantier" are tightly clustered into huge bouquets. The blooms are sometimes positioned high up at the top of the bush; the fragrance is reminiscent of that of vanishing cream. And at the height of summer, "Gloire des Mousseux," a moss rose, explodes in a riot of color. White, pink, or orange, bright red or purple, two-colored or variegated, there are flowers in abundance, such as those that bloom in Claude Pigeard's kitchen garden at Wy-dit-Joli-Village in the French department of Oise. There is a veritable deluge of blossoms and fragrances, including such varieties as "Mozart," a mass of crimson lake eglantines with a white heart, and the garden paths are enclosed by tunnels covered in rambling roses which tumble down to the ground in a wave of delightful fragrances.

"Pierre de Ronsard" is a jewel of a rose which blossoms in June and is a favorite with all French rose-lovers, delighting the eye with its deliciously delicate coloring, its charm as a climbing rose and its elegant shape, like the roses depicted in Persian miniatures. The borders contain "Comtesse du Barry" rosebushes, a classic rose of the old-fashioned type, whose pale gold blooms brighten the large expanse of dull green. The most opulent blossoms continue to flower into July, and they are then joined by the late-flowering varieties, some of which are unique of their kind. These include Colette's favorite, the "Cuisse de Nymphe" (nymph's thigh), whose English name is the far more chaste "Maiden's Blush." The very special hue of the foaming petals is reminiscent of the blush on the cheek of a modest young girl, and the delicate center of the flower, whose perfume is so captivating, has inspired poets since the fifteenth century. A rose with a strange name is the "Bizarre Triumphant,"

an exceptionally large, radiant bloom, whose impetuous flowers cover the range of purples and reds, from vermilion through chestnut brown. The whole warmth of summer seems to be embodied in a single flowering. Roses do not go on strike in August, yet it is often in September that the spring roses burst back into bloom with renewed vigor. One such rose is "Souvenir de La Malmaison," a classic, old-fashioned rose in all its perfection, which shades from the palest pink to ivory. It prefers a south-facing wall, and its tight petals open to emit a fruity fragrance. September is also the hour of glory for "Madame Isaac Pereire," which rambles over a ramp or long fence in bright sunlight. This exuberant rosebush drowns under a profusion of huge, strongly perfumed, generously ruffled blooms, whose amazing vigor extends to its luxurious foliage. The fall dresses certain rosebushes in purple or golden leaves, while others produce a mass of brightly colored rose hips. These can often be seen brightening the view along the freeway, where the bright vermilion fruits warm the heart and cheer the eye. This shows that certain modern rosebushes are perfectly able to cope with pollution, something that professional gardeners in city centers are well aware of—as seen in the resiliently colorful rosebushes that adorn our cityscapes.

There are even a few stubborn roses which defy the cold and still bloom at Christmas. This explains the name given to the "Snow Fairy" variety, whose virginal blooms with a touch of pink continue so late into the season. For many gardeners and garden lovers, the greatest wonder of them all is "Blush Noisette," a floribunda which looks lovely at any time of year. Only the sharpest frosts in the coldest of winters will wither its little bunches of flowers, which appear so delicate to the naked eye. In bud, they are pale lilac, but soon turn white, exhibiting golden stamens. They have a powerful clove-like scent, and when all the bushes are etched with a lacework of hoarfrost, all we can see are clouds of tiny, scarlet rose hips which brighten up the landscape…and which the birds find so delicious.

In André Ève's garden, which is open to the public, the rose-lover can come and choose from vast numbers of varieties growing in their natural surroundings (page 39). The old-fashioned types of roses he grows include "Long John Silver," a climbing rose with a wonderful scent whose pure white double flowers form large bouquets (facing page); "Blush Noisette," a tender, clove-scented variety which owes its name to Louis Noisette, a rose grower in the early nineteenth century who produced climbing roses that flowered repeatedly and were known as Noisette roses (top). The virginal pallor of "Iceberg," also known as "Snow Fairy," created by a German named Kordes, blooms in large elegant bunches (above).

Old-Fashioned Roses

"*N*o man knows through what wil centuries roves back the rose," wrote the English poet Walter de la Mare. The earliest type of rose was the eglantine or sweet briar. The fashion for cottage gardens has brought the wild eglantine back into fashion, as well as the other wild rose strain, the dog rose, *Rosa canina*, so called because it was once believed to have the power to treat dog bites. The sweet briar is a single flower whose five pink or white petals and five sepals surround a heart of yellow stamens. It grows on a hardy bush that is found in woods and whose crumpled leaves smell of green apples, as do those of the wild rose of the hedgerows.

"Old-fashioned" or "old-style" roses is a rather unscientific term. It actually covers a huge family of roses whose varieties and hybrids can be counted in their thousands. All, however, are the direct descendants of roses which are defined as "botanical." With a few rare exceptions, "old- fashioned" roses are those which existed in their present form prior to 1900. They are prized for the beauty of their shape when fully opened, combined with the wonderful fragrance they emit. They come in an astonishing variety of shapes and colors. There are cup-shaped or button-shaped roses, as round as peonies, some of whose petals are deeply imbricated, cabbage roses and roses with petals divided into quarters. The colors range from pure white to deepest red, via pink, mauve, and purple.

Among the oldest varieties are the Gallica roses (*Rosa gallica*, a rose that was cultivated by the Greeks and Romans), whose lovely flowers, with their chiffon petals, are strongly perfumed. Just before the rose fades, it takes on strange shades which are almost bluish-mauve. *Rosa gallica versicolor* was first recorded in the sixteenth century and is also known as "Rosa Mundi," allegedly in honor of Rosamond, the mistress of King Henry II of England, who is said to have been poisoned by Queen Eleanor in 1177. Its variegated petals are grouped around golden yellow stamens. There are other princesses in the rose family,

Semi-double roses (top) possess the simplicity of the eglantine and the delicate coloring of the old-fashioned varieties, whose corollas are so full that they split into quarters (above). This "Pierre de Ronsard" climbing rose will scale the highest walls and flower until the first frost (facing page).

such as "Belle de Crécy," whose petals change color from bright red to lilac, via pinkish-violet, depending on whether its petals are folded or exposed to the sun. "Tuscany" is a velvety, heavily scented rose, whose petals are violet crimson, with golden stamens glistening in the center of the flower.

The deep, heavy, frilly cabbage roses were the favorites of the Dutch masters who captured their abundant petals so perfectly in their still-life painting. In fact, the most famous of these roses has been nicknamed "the painter's rose." The elegant "Petite Lisette" has fresh pink corollas, the spectacular "Juno" bends under the weight of its iridiscent petals, and "Fantin-Latour" has the roundness and richness of a peony. They look even more wonderful in a garden and deserve pride of place there.

André Ève's garden, situated between Orléans and Fontainebleau, south of Paris, is at its best in sunny June, when banks of roses are offset by the brilliant green of the smooth lawns. The air is full of heady perfumes and the sight is glorious. Under the warmth of the sun's rays, the monochrome roses and lilacs, in reds and creamy white or ivory, velvety or smooth, are a stunning vision. The garden is famous for its hundreds of varieties of old-fashioned roses, whose numbers have been growing continuously for eighteen years. The catalogue published annually by André Ève grows ever bulkier. It is always consulted with great excitement by rose-lovers. "The advantage of growing old-fashioned roses," explains Ève, "is that they are easy to plant in a garden, they do not clash with anything, and combine beautifully with hardy perennials. If you plant a perennial one year before a rosebush they will live together for a long time in perfect harmony." He extolls the virtues of "Louis XIV," with its velvety crimson, almost black, petals, will flower in your garden for almost the whole summer. Then there is "Papillon": "Such charm and poetry resides in this rose, each of whose flowers is like a light butterfly alighting on the plant, whose pale pink petals are tinged with salmon."

The rose combines perfectly with other plants in delightful harmonies of color. Here in Provence, the white "Iceberg" blends with lavender, while in André Ève's rose garden, "Long John Silver" combines with the deep red blooms of a clematis (facing page). "Could there be a more delightful time to walk in the garden than in the early morning or late afternoon when the roses exhale all their perfumes!" writes the English designer Terence Conran. André Ève invites us to enjoy the perfumes of his rose garden (above).

Poulsen, the Danish rose-growing nursery, has produced a group of rosebushes called "floribunda," that are particularly hardy and robust, and able to adapt to the Scandinavian climate. They include the "Fredenburg" variety, its pink flower bursting with vigor and health (top). The cottage-style rose garden best responds to the current taste for a natural look. Against a background of climbing roses, the tall rose trees are surrounded by low-growing rosebushes, while a few hardy perennials supply notes of contrasting or matching color in blue and various shades of green (facing page).

Modern Roses

"I saw the sweetest flower wild nature yields, / A fresh-blown musk-rose; 'twas the first that threw / Its sweets upon the summer," wrote John Keats. But modern strains of rose would just as surely have won his admiration.

Tea roses (which originate from China and were imported into Europe in the tea clippers) have crossbred with other varieties, climbing or rambling. There is something "chic" about these types of roses. The flower is so lovely, the shape is handsome, and the perfume is like that of an herbal tea. The disagreements between those who favor old-fashioned varieties, with their perfumed grace, and those who like the hardy, modern, disease-resistant varieties which flower without fuss, goes back a long way. However, the success of the reflowering varieties (for which the correct term in English is the French word "remontant") and hybrid tea roses may have temporarily eclipsed that of the roses of yesteryear.

Subsequently—there is no such thing as a fashion that does not go out of fashion—tea roses were judged to look too stiff, too artificial, and sometimes they even became diseased like the old-fashioned roses. They thus gave way to the return of the old-fashioned kind. Contrary to persistent rumor, there are excellent old-fashioned roses that flower more than once, just as there are modern roses with a strong fragrance. There is no contest between old-fashioned and modern varieties. Just as kings used to marry off their daughters to make political alliances, today's rose growers, who operate in a high-tech environment, have solved the problem by creating roses whose blooms have an old-fashioned look and which are heavily perfumed, growing on strong and supple bushes, which reflower profusely and are also disease-resistant. This was the original principle behind the English rose varieties, and it is now applied to most of the latest creations. This is also the principle followed by of one of the leading English rose growers, David Austin, whose first creation, "Constance Spry" (1961), was named

for the leading florist of her day. It has large, double, cup-shaped flowers in a delicate, subtle, and luminous shade of pink, and a heady scent of myrrh. It is, quite simply, an "artificial" old-fashioned rose that is even more beautiful than the genuine article! "Heritage," also by David Austin, is another great classic from the same family. He himself considers it to be the perfect example of a bloom, in an irresistible pale salmon pink, with a delicious honey-and-flower fragrance.

The sumptuous "Abraham Darby" has enormous, full-blown flowers in a combination of pink, yellow, and orange, which have won universal acclaim. Its perfume is that of an orchard at the loveliest time of day, with an added touch of spiciness. André Ève finds "The Prioress" an exciting bloom: "The shape of this rose is so elegant! Its iridiscent white petals are cup-shaped at first, gradually opening to reveal long golden stamens. It should be pruned in such a way as to enable it to flower at nose height, so that the perfume can be smelled at its best."

Of course, English botanists have a wealth of experience and knowledge, enriched since the early seventeenth century by imports from the Orient. In the great tradition of the early-twentieth-century rose growers, such as Dickon or the Reverend Pemberton, David Austin began creating a magnificent collection of his own creations, which now consists of a hundred or so varieties which have nothing "old-fashioned" about them but their name. He is a true visionary, who foretold and anticipated the current fashion for those lovely roses of the past which bloomed in English cottage gardens and on country estates.

Peter Beales is another English rose grower who has exerted a considerable influence on taste in roses. He is one of the greatest specialists in old-fashioned roses and his opulent blooms are capable of creating a unique atmosphere of charm and harmony in any garden. Another major figure in the development of roses in Britain, was W.E. Harkness, who founded a rose-growing dynasty, and whose patient work has been continued for generations.

In 1961, David Austin first succeeded in crossing one of the old-fashioned varieties with a modern rose. This was the start of a long, fruitful series of new roses with big peony-like, open flowers and an elegant but powerful scent (facing page). "Leander," one of the best examples, has double petals that are arranged in the shape of a rosette. It is a glorious apricot color with strong, fruity perfume (below). "Graham Thomas," dedicated to one of the great English rose growers of the 1950s, is a brilliant lemon yellow color, and droops under the weight of its petals (bottom).

French Growers

The great rose growers in France also responded intelligently to the general enthusiasm for more supple, less conventional roses, whose gentle, fragrant shapes would revive the old-fashioned tradition in a riot of colors and scents. Thus Meilland created "Honoré de Balzac," named for the famous novelist, which has delightfully romantic flowers in a creamy white edged with the palest carmine pink and the subtle fragrance of ripe peaches. "Auguste Renoir," a hybrid tea rose as luscious as many of the paintings by its namesake, has huge pink flowers and is strongly perfumed, while "Toulouse-Lautrec" is an intense golden yellow against a background of lush, shiny foliage.

It is no accident that these contemporary roses have been named for the great French writers and artists of the nineteenth century. French rose growers are concerned to combine tradition with modernity in the richest possible range of "artificial" old-fashioned, but heavily perfumed, roses. Delbard is another grower who has created "artists' roses." These include the white, red, and yellow flames of "Claude Monet," the warm, light palette of "Paul Cézanne" with its scent of cinnamon, and the ruby peach, raspberry and wine lees coloring of "Paul Gauguin." "And just as the smell of a madeleine cookie dipped in tea so moved Marcel Proust in *Remembrance of Things Past,"* adds Henri Delbard, "the fragrance of 'Souvenir de Marcel Proust' is an invitation for you to take a walk in the garden of your childhood. In the morning, you find yourself in the kitchen garden, with its notes of pumpkin, at midday you are in the orchard with pear, peach, and apricot fragrances, and in the evening there are the musky notes of sandalwood and cedar, leading you into the shrubbery."

Jean-Pierre Guillot, whose name has been associated with rose growing for five generations, has paid homage to one of the great fashion designers of modern times, but has also responded to the demand by gardeners for old-fashioned types of rose. His "Sonia Rykiel," named for the leading fashion designer, offers all the elegance of a silky cup whose delicate pink petals shot with amber are soft and matte like chiffon. Recently, William Christie, the conductor of baroque music, inspired the rose grower. The rose which bears his name is as delicately perfumed and graceful as a rose of yesteryear. Christie is himself a keen gardener and rose grower. He has restored a small eighteenth-century farm in the Vendée, in western France, and created a garden of rare harmony whose profusion of roses combines with a carpet of lavender.

While it has always been traditional to name a rose after a leading personality, the world of fashion is directly involved when a rose grower, in this case Truffaut, is asked by a designer, in this case Christian Lacroix, to create a special rose. The result is a rose that is matte, changing, and lacy, reminiscent of flamenco and the bullfighter's cape, although it is also grown in plain yellow, fuchsia pink and orange, all of them warm tones to create a flower that is definitely born under a sun sign, and destined to flower from June through September. "Madame Figaro," in the words of her creator, Henri Delbard, "is an elegant and refined, maternal and distinguished rose-woman," a response to the "Elle" rosebush (from the Meilland nurseries), whose colors change as it flowers so that the range is complete!

If you love roses, all you need is a little daring. Fall is the best season to plant roses, but there is nothing to equal the delight of purchasing rosebushes that are already in bloom during the high season. Just imagine in your head the layout of your little private rose garden. Run through it in your mind, and try to visualize the garden paths, bowers, tunnels, and plantings. Compare the tints, textures, and the most suitable environment for the blooms you will purchase. Then start choosing again on the basis of a detail, a perfume or type of foliage that takes your fancy. Inhale the divine perfume of "Queen of Violets," with its extraordinary violet-purple hue. Admire this compact, remontant rosebush with its delicate, celadon green foliage, which reflowers constantly right through October.

"Grand Siècle" by Delbard has all the elegance and delicacy of an old-fashioned rose, whose typical perfume is enhanced by notes of strawberry and apple (facing page, top). "Kronenbourg" (facing page, below) was created in 1965 by Sam McGredy, from Northern Ireland, who is one of Britain's best-known growers. Meilland Richardier's "Charles de Gaulle" (below) has a striking mauve color, while "Charles Aznavour" (bottom) flowers abundantly and continuously.

"Ferdinand Pichard" is a remarkable French rose, created in 1921, which produces flowers right through September (above). It has a most unusual variegated coloring of carmine red lightly streaked with white. It has an old-fashioned rose perfume, and double cup-shaped flowers. A flight of steps outside a little house tucked away in a quiet, countrified corner of Paris, sunshine, and a rosebush in full bloom—proof that even in the heart of the city roses can flourish and delight the eyes (facing page).
"The rose is the perfume of the gods and joy of men It adorns the Graces at the blossoming of love. It is the favored flower of Venus."
"The nightingale sings to the rose The roses are blown by the breeze A moment then let us repose Our lives are as fleeting as these."
Anacreon

Waves of Perfume

"I think I am quite wicked with roses; I like to gather them and smell them till they have no scent left." Who could blame Maggie Tulliver, heroine of George Eliot's immortal *Mill on the Floss*? No other flower can rival the rose in fragrance. There are many other scented flowers that exist in nature, each of which has its own characteristic odor, such as lily-of-the-valley and violet, jasmine, and lilac. But the rose is a precious gem, whose hues are perpetually changing: it can produce scents of infinite diversity, which may be reminiscent of fruits or spices, lemon or vanilla, honey or rice flour, aniseed or apple, moss or patchouli…each scent is more intoxicating than the last.

The perfume of the rose is the result of complex alchemy. It is usually most heavily concentrated on the surface of the petals, so that roses with very thick corollas, that are half-open and generally brightly colored, are usually the most heavily perfumed. Their extraordinary richness of fragrance is often ephemeral and depends on a number of variable factors, including the weather (whether there is a breeze or utter stillness), the amount of sunshine or degree of humidity in the air, the time of day and the presence of another, parasitic odor, such as that of tobacco. One needs to take one's time with roses, visiting them over and over again, bending over them and retaining the scent that changes in intensity from one minute to another. The most sophisticated analytical techniques have been applied to the fragrance and have proved that it takes a total of nearly twelve hours for a rose to be able to emit all the notes that its fragrance contains. There are ephemeral headnotes, richer heartnotes, and a final trail of basenotes.

"I have perfumed my soul with the rose my whole life," wrote Guillaume Apollinaire, the French poet. Although silent, roses exist to speak a language, the universal language of sensitivity, feelings, emotion, and imagination.

Rose Bouquets

The red rose whispers of passion,
And the white rose breathes of love;
O the red rose is a falcon,
And the white rose is a dove.

But I send you a cream-white rosebud
With a flush on its petal tips;
For the love that is purest and sweetest
Has a kiss of desire on the lips.

J.B.O'Reilly, A White Rose

"Heritage" (opposite) is a classic
in the family of English roses
created by David Austin. The
shape is perfect and it has a
delicious, honey-scented
fragrance, two huge assets for
creating romantic bouquets
and arrangements.

"Papa Meilland" (above) is a true gem of a rose. It is a most unusual bloom, in the fullness of its shape, its powerful scent, and its rich velvety purple coloring which contains blue-black highlights. Henri Moulié is one of the very few Parisian florists to grow a large proportion of the flowers he sells at his store in the Place du Palais-Bourbon. An example of his work is this magnificent bouquet of garden roses (previous page), with "Pierre de Ronsard" in the background, "Heritage" in the left foreground, and the pale yellow "Toulouse-Lautrec" in the center.

If the natural habitat of the rosebush is the garden—as a fragrant bush or a natural-looking border, climbing a corner of a wall or rambling over a bower—it is nevertheless a fact that most people want to bring roses into their homes, to be able to experience their shapes and colors from as close as possible, to retain their perfume, to hold them prisoner for a moment in time. The way in which flowers in general, and roses in particular, are used, is an expression of the desire to please. Through the medium of a few roses, a little bouquet bought from the florist, a fragrant bunch picked in the garden, or a spray delivered by a messenger, there is a wealth of expression, from a token of affection, a thank you, a mark of acclaim or respect, from the most conventional good wishes to the deepest attachment.

Giving roses is a natural gesture whose meaning ranges from good will through deep desire: roses can be offered to others in order to please and attract, express admiration, affection, and love. Even though the giver is probably well aware that the pleasure roses offer is nothing if not ephemeral, such generosity is all the more justified since it also provides satisfaction for the giver. Succumbing to the attraction of a few fresh roses on the stall of a flower-seller in the market is one of the great pleasures in life. Even a single rose can be an inspiration. Gabriel García Marquez is well known for being unable to write a line without a yellow rose somwhere in sight.

The Dutch florist Marcel Wolterinck is a master of the art of contrast. Here he brings out the voluptuousness of the red rose by placing it in a simple pewter goblet (below). Jean-Luc Blais created this table centerpiece for the actress Claudia Cardinale. The dark green foliage sets off the crimson blooms (in this case, Colombian "Pharoah" roses) against a background of gold and velvet (bottom). "Leonidas" is a very fashionable rose for modern bouquets, with its distinctive, warm, appetizing chocolate-orange coloring (overleaf).

Foliage in the Bouquet

Legend has it that while Saint Dorothy was being tortured for her faith, an angel appeared to her offering a bouquet of roses to help her bear her sufferings. It is also said that she converted one of her executioners by sending him roses from Heaven in the midst of winter. If the peoples of Antiquity crowned themselves with wreaths of foliage and flowers when they attended a banquet or watched a gladiatorial combat in the arena, it was for religious reasons, in order to please the gods. But what was good for the gods soon became good for man.

Throughout the ages, even in Rome, the cut flower, and the rose more than any other, was a sign of luxury. When Cleopatra held a magnificent banquet for Anthony, the marble floors were covered 24 inches (60 centimeters) deep with rose petals held in place by invisible netting. The Muslims had a particular passion for the rose which the Crusaders adopted in turn. The rose has greater symbolism than any other flower. It was the most eloquent and the most sought-after flower of the Middle Ages. It is ever-present at civil and religious ceremonies, as well as in the world of fashion and beauty, from elegant accessories to everyday wear, from the "chaplet of the roses" to garlands and sprays arranged at floor level or gracing magnificent dinner tables. An Italian author of the Renaissance wrote of "a gray silken tablecloth on which were strewn white, scarlet, and crimson damask roses."

Yet at the time, nothing had been invented to enhance

Madame de Pompadour introduced a fashion for floral settings and liked to appear in a setting of roses, as in this portrait by François Boucher, painted in 1756 (below). The nineteenth century saw the invention of posy-holders (bottom). In the Parisian apartment shared by Chopin and George Sand, both of whom were wild about roses, bouquets, and rose-painted objects, are a reminder of their passion (facing page).

the appearance of roses that had been picked or cut: there were no vases, no side tables or pedestals. It was not until the seventeenth century and the introduction of the concept of interior design that the bouquet made its first true appearance. The word dates from the 1400s and is derived from the French word "bosc," meaning a wood or forest. In his *Histoire générale des plantes*, published in 1587, Daléchamps still felt a need to explain this new and strange custom whereby "flowers are packed into handfuls and placed in vases or painted china pots which are filled with water." This little collection of flowers soon became a favorite ornament which, by being produced in a surprising range of colors and shapes, rendered homage to the rose in a thousand different ways. Madame de Pompadour was responsible for the bucolic fashion for flowers on fabrics and walls in a supposedly rustic indoor setting, in which drifts of delicate roses took center stage. In the wake of the "Pompadour rose" came the fashion for real flowers used in sprays, as a corsage, worn on the shoulder, in the hair, or attached to a ribbon at the throat.

Say it with Roses

"Césarine was dressed in white crêpe, a wreath of white roses in her hair, and a rose by her side; she sent Popinot wild…." This maidenly portrait which Balzac paints in *César Birotteau* is the stereotype of an era in which young girls were wholly ignorant of life in general and love in particular, except in the coded, sentimental, and saccharine form of the language of flowers. It was a language spoken everywhere in Europe and for which the Americans conceived an overwhelming passion. It was a language that made it possible for the giver to create an encrypted bouquet which could be deciphered by the receiver. From absinthe (bitterness) to zinnia (unfaithfulness) via begonia (warmth) or petunia (obstacle), every flower sent a specific message. Only the rose could be interpreted in a number of ways. The centifolia rose meant "grace," and the moss rose "sensual

pleasure." The white rose meant "love which sighs," and was reserved for the (true) maiden and for the bride on her wedding day, while the red rose suggested "passionate love," the pink rose "lover's promise," and the yellow rose "infidelity." The pompom rose meant "kindness" and the Provins rose "patriotism." If the roses were full-blown, the message was clear, "A tryst, letter follows." But if they were dried, this meant: "Rather death than lost innocence."

Often considered to be pure silliness, the language of flowers, originally known as *selam*, first emerged from the harem of the Turkish sultan. It spread to Europe in the early eighteenth century through the letters of Lady Mary Wortley Montagu, a great traveler and letter-writer, who had discovered this mode of communication through petals in her visits to the seraglio. Reproach or quarrel, love, friendship, or passion, *selam* was capable of saying and interpreting everything. What remains of it today? Who still indulges in parlor *selam*? Our grandparents were probably the last to be initiated into its secrets. Apart from the gift of a dozen red roses, a message whose meaning persists, the language of flowers can be considered to be obsolete. Yet something of it survives, mainly in the colors. Red always signifies love, and white, purity. And now that florists are increasingly making use of brightly colored vegetables (peppers, cabbages, eggplant), fruits, seeds, and spices, there is nothing surprising about finding, slipped in among the red roses—meaning "madly in love"—a few red chili peppers, whose connotation is "torrid passion."

The Florist's Art

"Finally, she pushed open the door and after examining Jacqueminot and Maréchal Niel roses, carefully chose two perfect specimens of a new rose with a silvery hue, waited for the florist to wrap them in cotton wool and, to protect them even better, slipped their long stems into her muff." The novelist Edith Wharton thus sets the scene of an upper-class New York

The delicate, creamy tint of the inside of a shell, a sweet, pervasive perfume, an abundance of feathery petals in the corolla: that is the magic of the "Heritage" rose, created by David Austin, which has the form of an old rose, but which is more beautiful than many genuine old-fashioned blooms (facing page). "Maya" (below) is silvery white tinged with pale pink, and is a recent creation. It embodies the symbolism and fascination of perfection.

*Charm, freshness, and a natural look.
Whether in the country or in a
fashionable district of Paris, florists like profusion and an abundance of colors.
Tightly packed into little baskets in a "nest"
of dry twigs, these "Show Ballet" roses
take on a rustic charm (above).
Bunches and sprays are grouped in
profusion in Baptiste's store (facing page),
offering a palette of shimmering color.*

client shopping in a Broadway florist. Everything is there in this description: the choice of varieties, the demanding nature of the purchaser, the care taken by the clerk.

The birth of flower-selling as an art dates from the early nineteenth century. In Paris, Jules Lachaume was its most noble representative. He revolutionized the trade by publishing a treatise on arranging natural flowers. His store on the Rue Royale opened in 1845. Its decor is the same as it always was, pink marble, rockery, fountains and cherubs, a shrine to floristry in the Western world.

During the second half of the nineteenth century, life was not considered worth living without an abundance of flora in the home. "A flowerless room is a soulless room," claimed the writer and garden-lover Vita Sackville-West. Once a woman was married, the apotheosis of the blushing bride in a litany of white roses and orange blossom, daily life had to be filled with huge displays of flowers, in which the rose continued to play a major role. Flowers, especially roses, were the ultimate gift. The French actress, Sarah Bernhardt, loved to smother herself under armfuls of roses, and, according to a persistent rumor, was bribed by rose growers in southern France to promote the idea that carnations brought bad luck in the theater!

From 1860, the "rose trains" ran along the Bastille-Vincennes railroad line, bringing flowers to the wholesalers which were very much appreciated in the Paris region. Many of them came from the tiny village of Brie-Comte-Robert. A few years later, in New York, huge hothouses processed several thousands of plants in a streamlined fashion that was no different to any other business. The time had passed when people became ecstatic at the sight of a bouquet of roses in January.

But the abundance of roses was accompanied by new demands on the florists, those of naturalness and spontaneity in flower arrangements. Today, flower markets are the most popular places to buy flowers for the general public. They are a mosaic of color, the stalls are packed with healthy blooms. Whether in New York or London, at the great auction halls of Amsterdam or New Covent Garden, there is a multicolored harvest all year round.

Brilliantly colored, fragrant garden roses ensure that the smallest bouquet is a masterpiece of harmony. Even when combined with other flowers or plants, they remain the stars of the show (below, the elegant "Caprice de Meilland," the fresh, bright "Yves Piaget," the delicate "Pierre de Ronsard," and the mysterious bluish-mauve of "Charles de Gaulle"). Art blends with nature (facing page), when the deep pink "Yves Piaget" and the amber "Paul Ricard" (whose spicy perfume is reminiscent of aniseed) are arranged in front of a painting by Claire Basler.

In the late twentieth and early twenty-first centuries, Ecuador is emerging as the largest producer of roses, and flowers from South America appear in florists' stores all over the northern hemisphere as soon as the weather turns cold—a time when local varieties become rarer and very expensive. The climate of the Andes is ideal for rose growing and the buds produced are large, hardy, and very long-lasting. Tanzania, Zambia, and Kenya are also emerging as important rose-growing countries.

Despite this, the roses of the Paris region continue to enjoy an international reputation, and the hothouses are constantly being modernized due to that major obsession which so preoccupies rose growers and florists: the quest for novelty. In these shrines of glass, roses ready to deliver their harvest grow toward the light in a forest of long, straight stems, still greedily awaiting their splendors to come. The buds are cut as soon as the petals are visible, a delicate hint of the color they will display, but until recently this would have been considered a late harvest. It is not so long ago that the stores sold sprays of roses whose buds were tightly closed. Nowadays, no one would choose to buy buds. Naturalness is the order of the day. The roses that grace the modern interior need to look as though they had been freshly picked.

The Great Fashion for Roses

Just like the creators of "nouvelle cuisine," the "nouveaux" florists, most of whom are now male, have become celebrities in their own right. This important trend was started by an English woman, however, named Constance Spry, without whom the art of flower arranging might never have flourished as it has done. A wellspring of ideas for good housekeeping, she made her name in England in the 1930s and has now been immortalized for all time by David Austin, whose first rose, a rose in the old-fashioned style, created in 1961, is named for her.

Since the early 1990s, the rose has suddenly made a comeback, and is once again the height of fashion. The new

roses have interesting colors and shapes. Perhaps it was the reappearance of old-fashioned types in a new guise which sparked off the worldwide enthusiasm. At the time of writing, the rose is the most widely sold cut flower in the world, a testimony to its enduring appeal. In the U.S. alone, over a billion roses are bought every year.

Public opinion polls conducted in the Western world send the message loud and clear—the rose consistently comes out as the number one choice of flower for over 80 percent of those surveyed. Runners-up include the tulip, the carnation, the lily, the iris, freesia, and the chrysanthemum. Reflecting this enthusiasm, and uniquely in the history of floristry, stores have sprung up that sell nothing but roses. The first of these opened in Paris, in 1991. It is called Au Nom de la Rose (In the Name of the Rose) and is located on the rue de Tournon.

"Everyone's crazy about roses. In my opinion, people will start eating them one day!" claims Marlo Phillips, who was one of the first American florists to offer compact arrangements of roses in the shape of a ball. The Rosa Rosa store in New York sells more than three thousand bunches of a dozen roses a week, while Roses Only, another New York store, sells nothing but roses grown and exported from Ecuador, which are already in full bloom—because that is how people like to buy them, at the height of their beauty.

The new stars of the firm of Meilland—roses colored in white, red, pink, yellow, roses dotted with two colors, and even blue and lavender-colored roses—have been named "Folies." They are a bridge between the garden rose and the type sold by florists, since each stem bears between three and ten blooms, like home-grown floribunda roses. With the rapid expansion of the Internet, once exclusive flowers like these are now available on a plethora of sites. Whatever the time of year, the country, or the type of rose you are looking for, the Internet has the answer, with companies offering to send a red rose in an elegant box, a red rose with a bottle of champagne, accompanied by a message of love written in calligraphy on a piece of parchment, or even a rose made of the finest chocolate!

Au Nom de la Rose is a store that opened in Paris with the idea of attracting rose-lovers by offering them the essence, quality, and the scent of roses. It offers heavily scented, expensive garden roses produced by sixty thousand rosebushes in the Gard in southern France. These unique blooms have all the attractions of old-fashioned roses with rare colors and heady fragrances, such as this gorgeous symphony of red roses (facing page).
The understatement of the decor of dark wood and hammered zinc (above) emphasizes the fresh beauty of the famous "Yves Piaget" rose, with its eighty peony-like, ragged-edged petals.

To pay homage to the palette of the Impressionists, Guy Delbard created the "painters' roses," such as the delightful "Henri Matisse" (above), which is used by the best florists to produce magnificent arrangements. The flower may blossom in shades of white, pink, or red, and no two blooms are alike. "Serena" miniature roses are no larger than a fingernail, and yet they are genuine roses. The rose and stem never exceed a total length of 3 inches. The peculiar attraction of the miniature is seen here to full effect on a doll's armchair, with a Lilliputian trug basket of roses beneath it (facing page).

The Art of the Bouquet

At one time there was a greater preoccupation with shape than with color. A variety of single-color blooms were developed, a wider range of hues was introduced. Today, the opposite is true. Depth and contrast of colors, attractive, refreshing, and surprising hues are all the rage, right up to green roses, the latest curiosity. Shades are mixed without fear of clashing, and the decoration of the vase in these new arrangements is also an important factor. Roses have greatly benefited from this renewed interest in tones, which has slightly dented the image of the red rose and the single-color bouquet, since the fashion now is entirely for mixed tints in a single bouquet. As for the rules which once codified floral arrangements, these have now given way to spontaneity and imagination. Anything is possible, especially with roses, because old customs can be reinterpreted to give rise to new and daring arrangements, which sometimes are no more than fads.

All styles coexist, from the single bloom to the massive arrangement, from the modest country bunch to an elaborate artistic creation—structured or flowing, rustic or distinctive, minimalist or overblown. A single rose in a crystal vase is enough to trigger the magic. Whether they are garden roses, discovered behind a hedge or along a garden path, or the most elegant specimens purchased at the florist, all can be used in a flower arrangement of elegance and sweetness. Traditionally, it was always the graceful single tea hybrids, on their long stems, which produced the loveliest cut roses, and these were thus considered the most suitable to use in a bouquet.

But in truth, all roses, especially if they are scented, make the most wonderful bouquets, unique arrangements dictated by the location in which they are to be placed: here, a spray of long stems bearing white and yellow roses in a tall crystal vase, classical simplicity in all its elegance; there, a few old-fashioned roses in sweet-pea colors, a rather faded mauve, a dull pink, and a very muted orange, in a crackle-glaze pottery pitcher, a reminder of the past, set against the background of a lace curtain. Enjoy the undisputed charm

of a bouquet of lavender and crimson roses tied with colored ribbons, or the note of freshness provided by tiny pompom roses floating on the surface of the water in a green celadon bowl. Taste the tranquil luminosity of fragrant velvet "Aloha" roses opening in a glass bowl, or the very soul of the rose, in an armful of purple petals with an old-fashioned scent, floating in a stone basin.

Roses of the Florists

The major rose growers breed flowers on the basis of such criteria as their lifespan in the vase, the shape of the flower, the length of the stems, and the smallness of the thorns. They have concentrated for years on producing the ideal varieties for cutting and displaying indoors. The lifespan in the vase has lengthened considerably and can now be as long as two weeks. For arrangements that will last longer, it is best to choose roses that are still in bud—this is even more important in summer than in winter—but which are on the point of opening (when the first petals around the edge are beginning to spread apart). Do not choose buds that are too tightly furled, as these may die without ever opening.

One of the most important criteria for choosing the blooms is that of coloring, of course. This is a huge subject, in which fashion, in clothing, cuisine and interior decoration, is always a consideration. For example, "Maya," an iridescent white edged with pink, is currently one of the best-selling varieties, very much in demand, and with a promising future ahead, as has the aptly named "White Success."

"Léonidas" is another winner; its distinctive chocolate-orange blooms are so unusual that its appearance is always noticed. And then there is "Nicole," whose petals are edged with violet, to say nothing of the little "Tango," created as long ago as 1927, and still a favorite. This long-flowering rose is also known as "Gruss and Cobourg." It produces full, very fragrant flowers of a coppery orange color which is tinted with rose on the reverse side of the

"Madame A. Meilland" (facing page), probably the most famous French rose, lends itself to classic bouquets. "Toulouse-Lautrec" and "Pilgrim" have been arranged by Christian Tortu into a bright configuration (below), while four different hues are combined into an original garland (bottom).

*The "Marie Curie" has very bright orange
petals edged with pale pink (above).
At Comme une Fleur it is combined with a
poem by the French court poet, Clément Marot
(1496-1544), entitled "About the Rose."
"The lovely rose, to Venus dedicated,
The eye and senses with great joy provides;
I shall explain, O lady who delights me,
The reason why these roses are so red.
One day, when Venus her Adonis followed
Amid a garden full of thorns and branches,
Barefoot and arms all unprotected,
A rosebush pricked her with its piercing thorn;
Hitherto all rose flowers had been white ones,
But her blood now turned them deepest red.
And so this crimson bloom have I selected
Because this gift, far more than could be said,
Reminds me that your face preserved in sweetness,
Is reminiscent of this fresh, vermilion rose."*

petals. "Papa Meilland" and "Pierre de Ronsard" have been around for a long time, but their popularity shows no signs of waning. Their delicious perfume makes them invulnerable to the vagaries of fashion. On the other hand, "Noblesse," a weak pink, has lost all its attraction, as have "Mascara" and "Pavarotti," both of which seem to have fallen out of favor.

Today, the fashion seems to be for warm tints and brilliant colors. Yellow and orange have been among the most popular colors for years, even though red is still the most in demand. The Japanese, however, swear by the black rose. Almost all black roses are produced exclusively for the Japanese market, which means they are extremely rare in Europe. When they do occasionally become available elsewhere, it is at a price. Pale yellow roses were very popular in the 1950s, but fifty years later, they have been replaced by mauve in all its shades that, when combined, are extremely attractive and eye-catching.

Rose growers then intervened to find replacements for the colors and varieties that had fallen out of favor with florists and their customers. Currently, 570 varieties of roses are sold commercially, and another thirty or forty new varieties appear on the market every year. Rose growers maintain experimental hothouses in which they conduct their research on roses, because the creation of a new rose requires the utmost skill, expertise and perseverance, from selecting the parents to the final choice, involving insemination, harvesting, sowing, and the long wait to see what the final result will be. It takes around ten years for a hybrid to be perfected and ready for mass cultivation.

Garden Bouquets

For those who are lucky enough to have a garden in which they can grow their own roses, the pleasures are manifold. How delightful it is to be able to create flower arrangements using the roses growing in one's own yard! "For the amateur grower who wants to obtain roses that are suitable for cutting," advises the rose grower André Ève, "it is best to choose a special spot in the garden

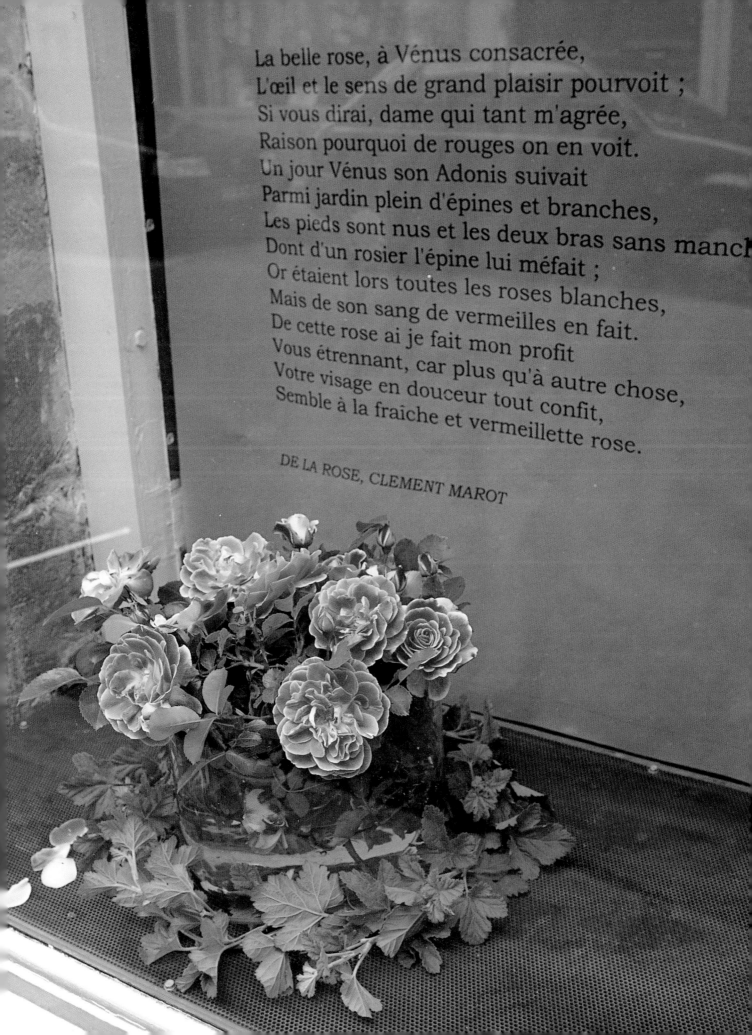

La belle rose, à Vénus consacrée,
L'œil et le sens de grand plaisir pourvoit ;
Si vous dirai, dame qui tant m'agrée,
Raison pourquoi de rouges on en voit.
Un jour Vénus son Adonis suivait
Parmi jardin plein d'épines et branches,
Les pieds sont nus et les deux bras sans manch
Dont d'un rosier l'épine lui méfait ;
Or étaient lors toutes les roses blanches,
Mais de son sang de vermeilles en fait.
De cette rose ai je fait mon profit
Vous étrennant, car plus qu'à autre chose,
Votre visage en douceur tout confit,
Semble à la fraîche et vermeillette rose.

DE LA ROSE, CLEMENT MAROT

where the roses can be grown so that when flowers are frequently cut from the bushes, they do not spoil the decorative effect of a bank of roses. The choice of variety is important. You must choose hardy bushes with strong stems and double flowers that are long-lasting. It is also a good idea to grow a few varieties that produce decorative rose hips in the fall, since these are very popular in fall and winter arrangements. Roses should be cut early in the morning, and preferably as soon as the buds begin to open. The cut blooms should be kept in water in a cool place until you are ready to create the arrangements."

Then comes the pleasant task of creating the arrangement. This may stem from a desire to produce something artistic or, more prosaically, from the need to produce a decorative item, but it is more often than not linked to a feeling of well-being and beauty that asks to be shared. Think of roses with petals as delicate as muslin opening in a simple pitcher, framed by a window that opens onto a garden. It could be the subject of an Impressionist painting. For a candlelit dinner party, arrange a few roses with velvety petals in custard cups on the table, and your guests will appreciate this delightful gesture. If all you have are a few lovely blooms whose creamy white petals are touched with a hint of crimson, trim them until they have virtually no stem and place them in a shallow bowl in the center of the table. The colors and scents of roses will be a delight for any room in the house, from the entrance hall to the drawing room, from the study to the bedroom and dining room.

Although the fashion is for bouquets that have a spontaneous look about them, avoiding anything conventional or strictly structured, you can also create your own minimalist arrangements with a little imagination and some unorthodox containers. Take an old soup plate or a painted metal window box or similar container and place three or four miniature jam pots, filled with water, inside it. Then let your inspiration run riot.

Roses are available throughout the year. In the garden, they begin to bloom in May, and flowering can continue until the first cold snap. During the winter months, roses

"Gather ye rosebuds while ye may..." These delightful "Pierre de Ronsard" roses seem to be ashamed of their roundness (facing page). French poet Pierre de Ronsard sang the beauty of the rose and thus amply deserves to have a rose bear his name (below).

*These bunches of roses evoke
remote corners of a country
garden in a vacation home,
where old pots are used to
accommodate a mass of
colorful blooms gathered
from the rose beds.*

The perfect combination of an embroidered tablecloth and a bouquet of full-blown roses blurs the frontiers between art and nature (below). "Toulouse-Lautrec" has dense, shiny foliage and all the charm of an old-fashioned variety, but with a luminous yellow color (bottom). Roses with large buds are cultivated in Ecuador. They are very long-lasting (facing page) and connoisseurs consider them to be the best in the world.

from the florist's take over. Seasonal colors can inspire your compositions. Pink roses with fresh greenery in spring, a combination of roses and freesias in a fragrant mass; warm, bright orange in the summer, with the communicative vitality of "Leander," an English variety with double petals and a fruity fragrance, whose vigorous lush growth is associated with the roses of India; ruby-red and crimson roses in the fall, combined with tufts of pink-and-purple heather; and finally, a snow-white rose in the winter, in which the purity and elegance of the pristine blooms are mingled with wreaths of variegated ivy.

But if you have a passion for pink, there are many other possibilities. For example, you can pack roses, cut just below the bloom, into a set of little tin boxes into which they fit very compactly. The leaves around the roses should be removed for best effect. You can choose the colors and the arrangement of the boxes, which can be kept together or arranged in a row. As an original single-rose arrangement, float a single pink, yellow, or red bloom in a transparent glass tinted in a matching color.

Everlasting Roses

The desire to preserve flowers beyond their natural lifespan has prompted the invention of a range of conservation techniques, some dating right back to Antiquity. The simplest of them is still used extensively, and it consists of suspending bunches of roses heads downward, in a warm, dry, dark, and sheltered spot. Another method, which was popular in Elizabethan England, consisted of burying roses in fine, clean sand, which was kept warm until the flowers were completely dehydrated. Today, silica gel is used to achieve the same effect.

In the days when most homes were heated by wood or coal fires, bouquets of fresh flowers had a short lifespan, and most interiors were decorated with arrangements of dried flowers which had to be kept under glass to preserve them from the woodsmoke, coal dust, and flying insects. Nowadays, more natural, less tortured arrangements are the

It is easy to make lovely arrangements with dried roses, provided you do not keep them in tight bunches while they are drying. Air must be allowed to circulate between the stems. Choose a warm, dry, dark place that is well-aired. When the roses are completely dry they become very brittle, so handle them with care (above). The blue rose does not exist in nature. Many rose growers have dreamed of creating a blue rose, but it continues to elude them, for the simple reason that the rose cannot produce blue pigment unaided, unlike the delphinium, forget-me-not, and many other flowers. However, thanks to a relatively simple procedure by which the rose is made to absorb colored dye, it is possible to create fresh roses that are bright blue in color.

fashion, and the glass dome has had its day.

The dried flower arrangement, like the fresh one, has experienced fads and fashions. Now that the fresh rose is back in favor with a vengeance, it was inevitable for the dried rose to make a comeback, and it has taken on its own importance, coming to the aid of the various evergreens, everlasting flowers, and sea lavender used in dried flower arrangements. Dried roses in faded hues are used to make arrangements, bouquets, wreaths, miniature trees, potpourris, and scented sachets, adding color and fragrance to all of them.

Air-drying by suspension takes one to two weeks to complete and is most suitable for rosebuds that are just about to open. It is economical and easy to do successfully. Do not make the bunches too tight, because air must be allowed to circulate between the stems. Choose a warm, dry, dark but well aerated place, such as a furnace room. Once the roses have been dried, they become very fragile, so handle them with great care. Excellent results can also be achieved by drying the flowers in a microwave oven, with the added bonus of speed. This works only for roses on a short stem. Cover the turntable with parchment paper or non-stick baking paper and arrange them carefully on it. Microwave on defrost, and check every twenty seconds, to ensure they are not damaged.

The use of silica gel (powdered silica crystals) is more complicated and time-consuming but works very well with full-blown roses, and preserves their colors. Pour a layer the thickness of an inch or slightly less (1–2 centimeters) into a container. Cut the rose stems an inch or so from the bloom and place the blooms in the gel with plenty of room between them. Cover with another layer of silica, sprinkled in a fine rain over the roses until they are completely hidden. Cover, and leave at room temperature for five to ten days. Carefully remove the roses and brush them with a soft paintbrush to remove any crystals that may have adhered to them, then thread them on florist's wire. After a few days, you can spray them with fixative or lacquer.

Not only can dried roses be used to create all kinds of elegant classical or modern arrangements, alone or in combination with other flowers, fruits, and foliage, but the petals themselves have been used to create striking pictures. The French artist Sofie Debiève arranges dried rose petals on paper. The petals have a rare subtlety and retain all of the texture and realism of the living plant.

If the dried rose, in every possible shade imaginable, offers a means of protecting the flower from the ravages of time, the "everlasting" rose, which is eternally fresh—and this is what makes it completely different—is like a mirage or magic trick. The principle is simple: the natural sap that circulates in the rose's veins is replaced by a colored sap which plays the role of the elixir of life. On the day the roses are picked, they are immersed in a liquid bath which they imbibe until they are completely saturated and none of their original sap remains. Sublimated by this miracle sap, radiant and glorious, the everlasting roses retain their supple, velvety petals for many years.

These blue roses are available from the delightful store in the Galerie de la Madeleine in Paris, owned by Rose-Marie Schulz. The blooms are treated with glycerin and dye, to make them "everlasting" and to color them.

This magical invention is applied to a flower picked the same day, and bursting with freshness. The rose is "sublimated" or "eternalized," becoming a choice accessory for florists and decorators. It is simply a matter of remplacing the natural sap in the rose with an artificial sap which the rose imbibes as soon as it has been cut, until it is gorged. Using these everlasting roses, designers can create cubic or rounded topiary work, planted in metal containers or vases.

Roses of Illusion

*A large rose-tree stood
near the entrance to the garden:
The roses growing on it were white,
but there were three gardeners at it,
busily painting them red. Alice thought
this a very curious thing and
she went nearer to watch them...*

Lewis Carroll, Alice in Wonderland

*Florence Maeght's interior design
store displays an incomparable
collection of fabrics, wallpapers,
and tapestries (right).
Michèle Aragon specializes
in the traditional Provençal
prints known as "boutis,"
including reproductions
of eighteenth-century flowered
cottons, which are washed
several times before use so that
the colors do not fade or run
(facing page).*

Florence Maeght's pillow covers (above) are decorated with traditional Provençal prints, from the pastel miniature rose to the cabbage rose, with a combination of various stripes. These gorgeous soft furnishings make it possible to create the loveliest atmosphere under the sign of the rose: the soft light of a crystal and wrought iron lamp delicately illuminates the stripes, bouquets, and garlands in this bedroom in which the bed and the cane armchair are an invitation to idleness (facing page).

The rose has been a favorite subject with artists and craftsmen, a decorative motif, since time immemorial, featuring on Persian carpets and Indian miniatures, mosaics and tapestries, then on printed fabrics and wallpapers, lace and embroidery, crude earthenware and bone china, and even on stamps. It appears on fashionable clothing, it is modeled in porcelain and reproduced on paper, silk, and glass. When Man first saw the rose, he was immediately inspired to celebrate it in all its forms, naive or stylized, realistic or impressionistic, in patterns, in friezes or in bunches. Nature herself contributed to this flowering of illusion, by using thousands of grains of gypsum to create sand roses, with their golden colors, flowering accretions that occur spontaneously in the most arid deserts.

The Artifice of the Flower

La vie en roses." Life in a world of roses is one of charm and beauty, color and sensuality. From the dawn of Antiquity, the rose has aroused passions and has played an important role in literature and painting, the applied arts and fashion. Young girls used to wear hats adorned with roses during religious processions and roses were often strewn during important festivals.

But it was not until the reign of Louis XV, king of France, that a fashion emerged for the bucolic and sentimental, involving the introduction of plants and flowers into all aspects of decoration. Under the instigation of Madame de Pompadour, the king's mistress, flowers were used extensively as motifs for china and glassware, furnishings, and clothing. Although carnations and peonies, lilies and irises were popular, roses were far and away the favorite flower.

Madame de Pompadour was painted by François Boucher in 1756 wearing a court dress which was covered with silk roses, with fresh roses strewn at her feet and on the little marquetry table she used as a writing desk.

Furnishings were transformed with the addition of swags and garlands of roses to their decor, in baskets, in bunches, in bouquets, sculpted in gilded wood on console tables, worked in marquetry on chests of drawers and writing desks, sideboards, and dressing tables.

Interior design, pillows and silk hangings, paneling and wallpaper became so heavily flowered that it was hard to distinguish between indoors and outdoors, whether one was in the drawing room or the garden. In fact, in November 1750, at a particularly opulent reception held at the Château de Bellevue, a property owned by Madame de Pompadour, who created the most elegant dishes and elegant surroundings for Louis XV, she is said to have entertained the king and his guests in a suite of rooms at the end of which there was a huge hothouse and a rose bed—and this during one of the bitterest of winters. In the hothouse, fresh roses predominated among carnations and lilies. The flowers so delighted the king that he repeatedly expressed his admiration for their beauty and their subtle perfume. Yet the vases of roses, carnations, and lilies, and even their stems, were made of porcelain, and the subtle odor of these divine flowers was merely the effect of their essences sprayed into the atmosphere. Nature had been so cleverly imitated that artifice was indistinguishable from the real thing.

This was the catalyst for the creation of all types of decorative conceits. Porcelain roses of great finesse and fragility were the original and exclusive specialty of a small pottery at Vincennes. Louis XV bought the factory and transferred production to Sèvres. Soon, the famous "Pompadour rose" was used on tableware and dishes, vases and candy bowls. China roses on metal stems were hand-modeled petal by petal, and constituted extremely costly items of decoration, arranged in vases and gracing the tables of the most expensive interiors.

This art has by no means been completely lost, and the fashion continues, even if the floral environment is not as omnipresent today as it was in the boudoirs of Madame de Pompadour. The famous porcelain flowers that were sold at incredible prices by "draper-merchants," forerunners of

Sometimes very little is needed in order to create an illusion, and mirror effects can be used to reflect onto the rose-patterned tablecloth the full-blown blooms that have just been picked in the garden (facing page). Fragile porcelain roses with wonderful petals of infinite delicacy have been an important element in interior design since the eighteenth century for table centerpieces and tableware, imitating the freshness of natural bouquets. The best of them today are made by artist Didier Gardillou, who uses the traditional techniques of the Vincennes porcelain manufactory (below).

today's antique dealers, in eighteenth-century France, are still made in exactly the same way using the traditional methods by a contemporary artist, Didier Gardillou, whose work can be admired (and bought) at the shop inside the Musée des Arts Décoratifs in Paris. These fragile creations take long hours of work, especially the assemblage of the delicate petals, each of which must be attached individually. The same delicacy of execution can be found in the glass roses which have long been made in Germany and in Bohemia, now in the Czech Republic.

In the case of crystal, the art of glass-making owes much to jeweler René Lalique, whose factory at Nancy produced the most exquisite Art Nouveau shapes for perfume bottles. Among his creations there are the full-blown flowers of Rose de Noël, a fragrance by Caron, or the naive patterns of little briar roses which decorate the flower-shaped bottle of Cœur Joie, the first perfume created by Nina Ricci.

The firm of Guillet has specialized in artificial flowers for the past hundred years. It creates exclusive artificial roses of rare quality and bouquets of unique elegance which it exports as far away as Japan. It has been brilliantly successful, but in a more accessible range, there are fabric roses imported from China (above). Emilio Robba creates his illusions with such artistry that it is almost impossible to distinguish them from the real thing without touching them. His brightly colored roses in a combination of shades, from mother-of-pearl to scarlet, imitate the matte, slightly irregular surface of freshly picked sprays of roses (facing page).

Silk and Cotton Roses

Many other materials and techniques have been used to enrich the craftsman's palette with floral illusions like those everlasting bunches of roses. Nowadays, there is not an interior design store, a soft furnishings department of a department store, a magazine article on an interior, that does not display artificial roses, whether as single-stem blooms, alone or in lavish bouquets, in balls or miniature trees. The fake rose, like the real one, is now the height of fashion and every type of interior succumbs to its charm, from floor to ceiling and in every possible shade and hue, to add pink to bedrooms, and coral, salmon, or pink madder, or even yellow, virginal white, or deep carmine to drawing rooms. Sometimes colors are used which were never seen in the garden, such as indigo or even violet. Further liberties are taken in the form of strident colors or simply unreal ones, such as the massive gold-dipped bouquets which the firm of Sia sells for Christmas.

The workshop at the firm of Légeron, founded in Paris in 1880, is still to be found in the Rue des Petits-Champs. It has retained the original shopfittings, the massive wooden counters with their deep drawers, the cardboard boxes, catalogues, and old labels, all reminiscent of dry goods stores of the distant past. Every available space is littered with wreaths, bouquets, and corsages of every shade and hue, ready to be packed in tissue paper and sent to adorn some designer creation.

The art of the artificial flower is pursued nowadays in creations of astonishing reality. One of the art's leading exponents is the French craftsman, Emilio Robba, whose creations—which are displayed in the Galerie Vivienne in Paris—are known and appreciated worldwide, particularly in Japan and the United States. Every year, Emilio Robba designs unique collections of artificial flowers, vases, candles, room fragrances, rugs, and lamps. His flowers, among which the rose is superbly represented, are made of cotton, silk, and even polyester, then assembled and painted by hand, and combined with real, stabilized foliage. They are then steeped in "water" that is eternally limpid and clear, a mixture of transparent resins. The silky transparency of their petals, the velvety buds, and suppleness of the stems, are so true to life that they are almost hyper-real. This perfection is also translated in the use of real flowers, such as a genuine rose which he imprisons inside transparent paraffin wax to create an exquisitely perfumed candle.

Many other designers use the rose in their products. Hervé Gambs, for example, uses all types of rose arrangements, including balls and sprays, bouquets, trees, and baskets. He also makes artificial perfumed rose petals, which are made of a special fabric designed to absorb the fragrances with which they are sprayed. He even creates fireworks that explode into rose petals. These are table decorations in the shape of a bomb. Once the wick has been lit, the "bomb" explodes and a mass of white or multicolored petals is shot to a height of 10 feet (3 meters) and showers down upon the guests.

Couture Roses

The divine "merchants of fashion," who were besieged by society women begging for their advice and their services, were as famous in late-eighteenth-century France as are the great couturiers today. The thousand and one frivolities with which they adorned their outfits included winding strips of roses as edging for

the skirts of dresses and rose hair ornaments, sprays of roses in the hair and corsages in the cleavage. These were created from beautiful artificial roses made from silk or velvet, paper or parchment. China has always been famous for its artificial flowers and has a long tradition, which was copied by the Italians. They used feathers, canvas, and even silkworm cocoons to imitate the velvety texture of rose petals. The French perfected this art by inventing all sorts of suitable instruments for cutting out, die-stamping, printing, and coloring artificial flowers.

On the eve of the French Revolution, in 1789, Paris had a dozen manufacturers of artificial flowers. There is a famous anecdote recounting how the famous Wenzel, who hailed from Bohemia, made a rose for Marie-Antoinette that has remained legendary. It was cut entirely from the thin membrane inside an eggshell and was disturbingly lifelike.

Slightly crushing their floppy silk petals, these infinitely delicate blooms, which the artifice of fabric renders divinely elegant, evoke the unique grace of old-fashioned roses whose names are so evocative, such as "Assemblage of Beauties," "La Belle Sultane," "Mousseline," or "Perpétuelle mousseuse." And yet they are manufactured by Légeron with consummate art, in order to adorn a corsage or a hat, a cocktail dress, or an off-the-shoulder evening gown.

To achieve the correct shading of a rose, the master flower-maker consults his color creation formulas. The petals are dipped in small bunches in a carefully concocted mix of dyes (below, inside the Légeron laboratory). There are valuable rose color charts (bottom). This is how an inch or two of muslin becomes transformed into a glorious bloom (facing page).

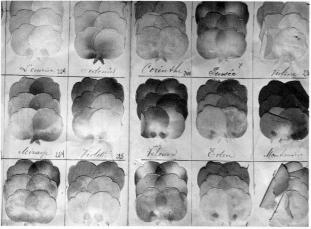

In time, the manufacturers of "flowers and feathers" increased in number. Even after World War II, there were still 277 workshops in Paris that described themselves in this way. A few of them have survived the vagaries of fashion, thanks to their innovation and reinvention of the image of the artificial flower, which is light years away from the cheap, plastic roses to be found in every hardware store, and marked "made in Hong Kong."

The atmosphere in the Légeron workshops in the Rue des Petits-Champs in Paris would appear to have hardly changed for centuries, and the archives of the firm contain those valuable color charts with their infinite gradations of color. In the hands of the experts, roses with pale gray petals and velvet leaves are created for Dior, requiring skills of rare complexity. Each rose consists of petals of different shapes and sizes, and the colors are shaded from the edge to the heart of the petal.

The firm of Lemarié, founded in 1880 by a woman who was herself a trimmings-maker, also creates artificial flowers for deluxe ready-to-wear and haute couture. Its great specialty is the Chanel camellia, but the rose also flourishes, in muslin or percale, in poplin or organza, constantly reinvented from nature in order to discover the subtle color gradations of swollen blooms, which are crimped, rounded, cleverly colored, and assembled.

Madame Lubrano, the granddaughter of the founder of the firm of Établissements Guillet, is in charge of production today. The magic is the same, but this time there is a certain element of flair and audacity that is often startling and spectacular. Guillet is the unofficial "florist" to Christian Lacroix, Nina Ricci, Thierry Mugler, and Sonia Rykiel, and is as creative in its roses made for interior design as it is in its fashion roses. For example, the firm produced five thousand silk roses which were worn by Estella Warren, in her role as an imaginary Eve created by Jean-Paul Goude for the launch of the perfume Eden by Cacharel.

It is artists of this quality who create the extraordinary floral arrangements that are seen on the catwalk in the millinery of the English couturier Alexander McQueen or

*Once treated,
the rose petals
are annotated,
described, then
filed in catalogues,
thus becoming
irreplaceable archives.*

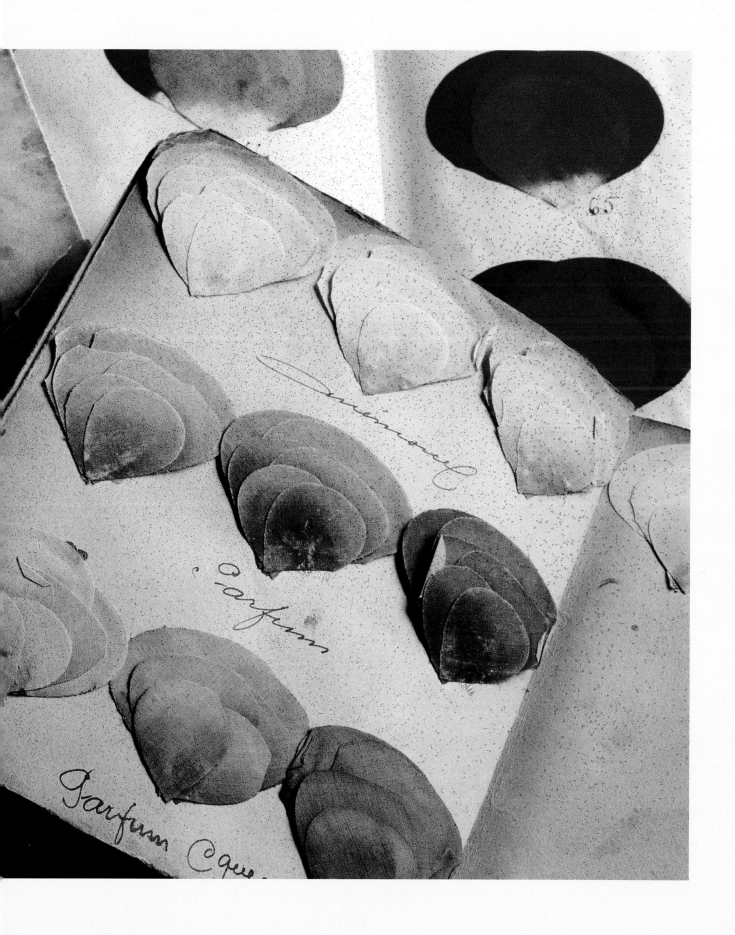

the "object-dresses" of the Italian Franco Moschino. An example of the latter is the strapless dress in the shape of a bouquet of fabric roses, in every shade of pink and red, which the model wraps in a sheath of cellophane.

The lifesize artificial roses, imitating May or Bengal roses, in tulle or velvet, silk, nylon, raw cotton, brocade, or even in leather or denim, that are displayed on the accessory counters of the department stores or certain specialist outlets, have created a place for themselves as adornments in the ready-to-wear clothing market, as an enhancement of elegant apparel or the last word in fashion.

On another level, roses can also be worn modestly and discreetly, in the form of tiny rosebuds, no bigger than the nail of a little finger, made of rolled satin ribbon in pale colors. The really minute buds are used to adorn a baby's bonnet or the crossover between the cups of a brassiere. If there is one type of clothing in which the rose predominates, it is indeed in lingerie, in its most natural representation, in satin, silk, and lace, an eternal allegory of the woman and the rose, in which the rose and the silk ribbon, two accessories that are inseparable from coquetry, are combined in the same sensuality. Since Antiquity, a silent dialogue interwoven with symbolism has existed between the rose and the feminine ideal. "The rose," said Rainer Maria Rilke, "…distributes this troubling scent of saintly nakedness."

Fashion Roses

Once upon a time, brightly colored, flowered cloth from India, Persia, and Siam was widely imported into Western Europe. Local manufacturers of silks and wools protested so strongly that these imports were eventually prohibited. The immediate consequence was that the cloth continued to be smuggled in, or that crude copies were produced locally, since fashion had not changed and tastes remained the same. Shortly thereafter, in the early eighteenth century, at Mulhouse

Peeping out of the tissue paper which delicately parts to let them through, these artificial roses are made of fabric and have been created, petal by petal, molded, rounded, and veined, so as to ensure that the illusion is perfect (facing page). Sometimes an understated rosebud, the color of an iridescent shell, will add a touch of refinement to an off-the-shoulder creation (below), or one might prefer a corsage of silky blossom the same color as the garment worn (bottom, rose on the author's wedding dress, created by Trousselier).

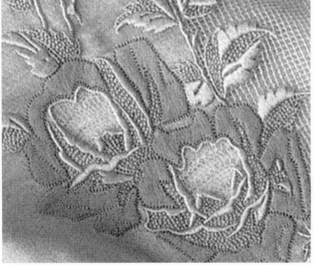

(now in France, but then in Switzerland), three young entrepreneurs founded the first local factory making Indian-style cloth. The same thing happened in Paisley in Scotland, which is why these copies of Indian patterns are known as paisley. Thousands of samples of such early examples are preserved in a museum of fabric printing in Mulhouse. They are a riot of exotic or wild flowers, bouquets and garlands, in which the rose features prominently. The cloth has been made up into skirts and shawls, scarves and mattress covers, much of it lavish reproductions of the local flora.

In fashion and ready-to-wear clothing, printed fabrics are certainly the most fertile ground for reproducing flowers in general and roses in particular, no matter what the style, material, or purpose of the cloth. Even before the birth of Art Deco, a high point for rose designs, the painter Raoul Dufy created rose-decorated labels and invitation cards for the couturier Paul Poiret. Dufy went on to create fabric designs printed with roses and peonies. He later worked with the house of Bianchini-Férier on a number of models, in which the rose, singly or in a bunch, was a recurring theme. In addition to printed fabrics, roses have been used in appliqué work and beading of every type, especially in the creations of Jeanne Lanvin or Jeanne Paquin. Pierre Balmain has produced some of the loveliest expressions of the rose in haute couture. He has also created numerous costumes for movies, and included among his celebrity clients the movie star Carroll Baker, for whom he designed a figure-hugging, transparent dress, entirely embroidered with roses, to which a voluptuous cascade of white tulle roses was appliquéed as strategic cover.

In the early 1960s, the first manifestations of "flower power" began to emerge on university campuses in America. This was a true liberation movement under the sign of the flower. Imagination and free love were promoted, as were equality of the sexes and a return to nature, all heavily laden with symbolism. In addition to the daisy, the signature flower of the 1960s, the rose continued to flourish, no longer as the voluptuous cabbage rose of romantic bouquets, but the little briar rose, the eglantine of country lanes. It now flowered on Cacharel dresses and blouses in the spirit of the flower patterns on fine Liberty cotton prints. The rose theme is still to be found in the collections of Agnès B., "Under the sign of the rose," although this designer is more often associated with stripes and black-and-white contrasts.

In addition to rose prints—much favored by the British designers Vivienne Westwood and John Galliano, who make good use of antique sprays and patterns—roses are often used in modern embroidery and appliqué work. Roses are embroidered in silk or cotton thread, in wool or lamé, motifs are worked in pearls or sequins, on the narrow boleros of Christian Lacroix, for example, or the soft linen skirts of Dries van Noten, on which the full-blown blooms are reminiscent of the bright patterns of Ukrainian folk costumes or the paseo capes of the bullfighters in the sand of the bullring.

In France, the Queen of the May was known as "une rosière" because she was crowned with a wreath of roses. Roses are still worn on the head, but currently as hats created by such milliners as Marie Mercié, who adds them as a border or in a single bloom. The extravagant creations paraded at fashionable racecourses, such as Ascot or Chantilly, have given designers the opportunity of making ample use of the rose. The picture hats, entirely covered with dozens of silk roses, that Philippe Model creates in his workshop are evidence of a spectacular refinement and elegance which gives the rose an opportunity to appear in all its glory.

Rose Patterns on Fabric and Paper

In the late eighteenth century, all Europe bowed to French fashion, and slavishly copied its trompe-l'oeil flower decors, dominated by pompom roses and eglantines, cabbage roses or centifolias. Whether in Prussia or in Russia, in London or Berlin, fabric

Silk, muslin, or satin roses are used to decorate every type of garment. They come into their own in particular in intimate apparel (facing page top, a Sabbia Rosa model), in all the subtlety of embroidery and lacework (facing page below, a pillow cover in re-embroidered faded rose silk created by the firm of Porthault in the 1950s). Philippe Model places a spray of silk roses on his fine straw hats (above top), and garlands of roses are embroidered across the panels of this taffeta corset with thin shoulder straps created by Max Chaoul (above bottom).

manufacturers produced lengths of light percale cotton or heavy silk brocade, painted fabric or paisley, cotton or silk prints, since textiles are the best way of reproducing this floral expression. Earlier, the invention of wallpaper, another major innovation of the eighteenth century, expanded on the fashion for tapestry or fabric wallhangings.

This is the realm of wallpaper and soft furnishing fabrics, destined for curtains, armchairs, and sofas, pillows, comforters, and bedspreads. Since the second half of the eighteenth century, the fashion for "imaginary" or "fantasy flowers" has never waned; they have invaded every type of interior. There have been many changes of fashion, but roses have continued to reign uninterruptedly, in an infinity of compositions, beribboned or suspended, braided or entwined, in vases, in bunches, or in little posies, in rows, bushes, or repeat patterns. Today, all styles coexist, whether naive or romantic, high or late Victorian, hyper-realistic or stylized. Mauny, a French manufacturer specializing in reproducing old wallpaper patterns, has made the most delightful recreations of the past, such as the delightful "Rose de France" pictured opposite.

The catalogues and collections of the designers and manufacturers lead us along flower-strewn pathways in which the creative imagination constantly returns to the rose. Baskets of roses and ribbons in various shades of blue are painted on thick canvases the color of terracotta, like frescoes on a sunny wall. Huge, brilliantly colored bouquets flower on glazed cotton. There are also simple chintzes on which graceful stems bear little roses with variegated petals.

Liberty, the London department store, reproduces the themes beloved of William Morris on linen, in which birds warble amid briar roses and strawberry plants. The store also favors cotton embroidered with magnificent five petaled roses. Lelièvre, a furnishing fabrics store, created a collection entitled "Allons voir si la rose…," ("Beloved, let us see if the rose," a quotation from the poet Ronsard) and offered a range entitled "Mignonne," including an

The delicate modeling and bright coloring of this English rose was reproduced on china cups for Whittard's of Chelsea in honor of Mother's Day (above top). It expresses the gracious modesty of the flower, while the wallpaper dating from the 1850s (above, a David Soyer pattern in the Musée de Mulhouse) evokes a profusion of greenery cascading beneath the roses. Mauny specializes in reprinting old patterns on the basis of contemporary color plates, creating rolls of period wallpaper which need to be carefully matched at the join (see the example on the facing page).

Mauny also creates border friezes (right, the famous "Rose de France" pattern). Like patterned wallpaper, these friezes must be printed with one block per color and per design.

ottoman embroidered with little roses, "Belle dame," a brocade fabric evoking a rose tree covered in butterflies, and "Milrose" silk curtaining patterned with armfuls of intertwined roses.

Since 1752, the firm Prelle has specialized in the manufacture of fabrics destined exclusively for furnishing the stately homes of France and museums throughout the world. It has an amazing range of sculptured velvet, silk brocade, gold and silver cloth, damascene, and other types of printed silks, in which the rose features in compositions of infinite elegance. Prelle is the only company which has continued to work since the mid-eighteenth century on the production of the most complex weaves. It is capable of reproducing the design, texture, and colors of fabrics that were used to decorate the most prestigious interiors, such as the queen's rooms at the château of Fontainebleau or the Vanderbilts' summer residence at Newport, Rhode Island, as well as castles in Scotland, England, Germany, and Norway.

Prelle's headquarters in Paris are in the very lovely Place des Victoires. The company supplies historic reproductions of the most prestigious historic fabrics. It has provided them for the Marble Palace in Potsdam and Louis XVI's bedroom at Saint-Cloud, and made fabric in the Napoleon I or Napoleon III style (facing page and below).

The French firm of Porthault has always loved flowers, and this example of its work consists of hand-embroidered openwork appliqué roses on a tablecloth (below). From a plain white piece of cloth, table and household linen has evolved and has become a palette for delightful designs in which rose stems are scrolled and entwined among rose leaves and rosebuds.

Yet the rose is not merely an adornment for Louis XV candy dishes and boudoirs, for English chintzes redolent of afternoon tea, an open fire, lavish garlands, and romantic baskets of roses against backdrops of figured velvet or stenciled paintings suitable for a young girl's bedroom. The rose can also take on more modern, and more daring, aspects. The Hill House near Glasgow, the masterpiece created in 1902 by the Scottish architect and designer Charles Rennie Mackintosh, is a brilliant illustration of this trend. He used a stylized wild rose as the principal theme for the decoration of the house, applying it to the bedroom walls and the drawing room which overlooks a rose garden, creating straight lines of friezes as if the roses had been trained over a trellis or liberally sprinkled in a repeat pattern. However the motif is treated, in wallpaper, as colored glass in the windows, or in stucco, it has the purity and originality of genius.

If the rose has been allowed to blossom freely on

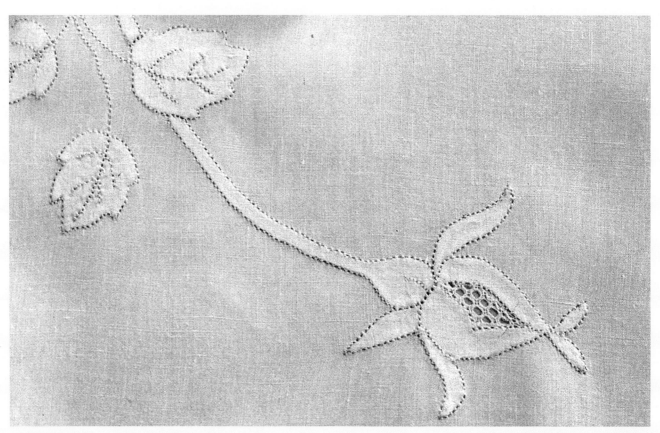

wallpaper, fabric-covered walls, and tented ceilings, it has also slipped into beds and onto tables, symbolizing all the metaphors of style and taste. From the petit point embroidered pillow, to the European-style cover for comforters and the best tablecloths, from the guest towel to bedcovers and from hangings to floral printed table mats, the rose offers its multitude of petals and pretty foliage, its full blooms and tiny, barely opened rosebuds. The Chinese invented a painstaking technique called "needle painting," which was introduced into France in the eighteenth century. Nimble-fingered embroiderers were able to reproduce on tablecloths designs of exquisite freshness with all the delicacy and finesse of real flowers. An example is the famous "Josephine" tablecloth created by Siècle, and decorated with a garland of Redouté roses. It is named for the Empress Josephine, wife of Napoleon I, who was passionate about roses. On a much more modest scale, far from the dining rooms of the rich and famous, paper serviettes are now models of elegance. For instance, there are those created from the collections of the loveliest fabrics from London's Victoria and Albert Museum, such as the "Fairy Rose Cream," worthy of accompanying the finest china.

Rosebuds in a semi-naive style used to feature on wallpaper considered suitable for young girls of good family (above, based on an original by Jane Churchill), and they still flourish in the creations of today's stylists such as Agnès B. Painters on porcelain often chose roses as a favorite theme, as if to combine the art of the table with the ephemeral nature of a bunch of flowers (below, eighteenth-century Sèvres porcelain cup and saucer).

Porcelain Roses

Since the middle of the eighteenth century, pottery and china have become favorite media for the most varied representations of roses, from Sèvres to Marseille, from Vincennes to Chantilly, from Crown Derby to Royal Doulton, on vases and cachepots, soup dishes and pomanders, cups and saucers. "Rosebuds and full-blown roses, in isolation or in groups appear in turn between the *apéritif* and dessert, at teatime and dinnertime. There are the roses with the perfume of childhood, whose fragrance we would so love to be able to find again today." These words are inscribed on the plates in the set of Limoges tableware called "Histoire de Roses," created by the famous decorator A. Raynaud.

Flowers have always been the favorite subject of artists, and the arts of the table have naturally been included in this inclination. Painting and stenciling on pottery, earthenware, porcelain, and bone china has often included roses, which have adorned dishes and plates, cups and sugar bowls, as well as coffee cans and pillboxes. The fashion for realism influenced this decoration from the late eighteenth century. Branches and repeat patterns of cut flowers were used to decorate objects. The floral motifs later became more sophisticated, with gilt outlines and rims.

In the late nineteenth century, the richness and fragility of full-blown roses were superbly represented on fine china, as in the "Eugénie de Montijo" pattern, created by the Bernardaud porcelain factory, which was offered as a gift to the Empress Eugénie, wife of Napoleon III, when she inaugurated the Universal Exhibition in Paris in 1867. Bernardaud now makes a modern service called "Aux Roses," which is sprinkled with rosebuds and open roses between friezes of laurel, while on the "Bois de rose" plates, scrolls interspersed with rosebuds evoke wrought ironwork in which little rose trees are depicted.

The Haviland pottery commissioned Nall, a pupil of Salvador Dalí, who in turn was inspired by Albrecht Dürer's etching *Roses of Tuscia*, to produce a very different type of work. The roses are extremely accurately reproduced in black and white, the fantasy accentuated by trompe-l'œil effects. The model represents the metamorphosis of a rose from one piece of china to the next, from its birth as a bud until its death, a faded flower that contains a promise of renewal because it has metamorphosed into a fruit.

Petit Point and Other Types of Needlework

During the nineteenth century, birthday and anniversary cards, invitations and valentines as well as all types of cut-outs, such as "penny plain and tuppence colored" images, were all the rage with the

During the Renaissance, the custom arose of strewing flowers on the table during a meal. In this modern version of the custom, it is the china that is rose-covered, alternating with real flowers in contrasting colors, showing that flower-decked tableware and dishes, such as this painted glassware by Despalles in the romantic spirit of Redouté roses (facing page), are still the height of fashion. As for cups, roses are a natural choice for a border or wreath. English painted china, Derby (c. 1802, top), eighteenth-century Sèvres porcelain (above right), and china from the Nantgarw pottery works in Wales (c. 1910, below).

Paper and tapestry wool for embroidery on the theme of roses. Below are paper plates and paper serviettes from the Victoria and Albert Museum, London. Bottom: petit point kit for embroidering pillows and rugs from Casa Lopez, based on watercolor paintings by Isabelle Valke. Throughout the ages, flower painters have been fascinated by the colors and shapes of roses (facing page, watercolor by Colette Renault).

Victorians. Many of these were decorated with charming posies, in which the rose had a worthy place. Rose bouquets were depicted, grasped in the chubby hand of a child with rosy cheeks and blond curls, or arranged in a small spray inside a cornucopea inscribed with the word "Affection."

The arts of tapestry and canvas needlework, embroidery and petit point have always followed fashion, from the medieval massed flowers on a dark background to Art Nouveau and Art Deco roses, via beribboned baskets in the Trianon style, inspired by the château of Versailles. As a theme to decorate pillows, armchairs, and footstools, needlework frequently featured a thousand and one variations on the theme of the rose, as the focal point, blossoming in the center of a square pillow, as an old-fashioned frieze, or in cross-stitch patterns.

The rose has blossomed on fans and candy boxes, wall tiles and coral pins, decorative boxes, and the binding of valuable books, enameled gold watches, snuffboxes, "millefiori" paperweights, Venetian lace, late Victorian papier mâché and early-twentieth-century barbola work. This imaginary museum of the rose should also feature the series entitled "Roses de France," designed by Émile Gallé in the early 1900s, including a flask called "To the languishing rose," in hammered and engraved crystal glass. After Art Nouveau, the style continued in Art Deco, with angular roses made of ivory inlaid in a walnut bed frame made by Leleu, or the roses in pewter and celluloid, made by Marie Laurencin on Macassar ebony chairs designed by Ruhlmann.

The rose will always be a source of perpetual surprise and delight to the poet and artist, as in this poem by American poet Emily Dickinson:

A sepal, petal, and a thorn
Upon a common summer's morn,
A flash of dew, a bee or two,
A breeze
A caper in the trees,
And I'm a rose!

Roses and Perfume

*What's in a name? That which we call a rose
By any other name would smell as sweet.*

*William Shakespeare,
Romeo and Juliet, Act 2, Scene 2*

*The lacy petals of "Yves Piaget"
(Meilland Richardier) emit
a perfume of rare intensity,
striking even to the
untutored nose (right).*

The painter John William Waterhouse *(preceding page) tried to capture the perfumed essence of the rose. It is the heady fragrance of the Bulgarian rose that predominates in Diorissimo, a perfume launched by Christian Dior in 1956 in a limited edition Baccarat crystal flask topped by a bronze bouquet of roses (below). This is also the rose which languorously wafts in topnotes over Private Collection, launched by Estée Lauder in 1972 (facing page).*

There are roses that are heady and triumphant, others that are fresh and sharp. Some exude an odor of moss and damp earth, others have a fragrance of spices and precious woods. Some white roses hide within their silky petals an aniseed note, whereas those of a crimson velvet tempt you to bite into the flower to discover the taste of raspberries. Some magic blooms conceal a perfume of clove and nutmeg, while others exude the odor of musk or of face powder, with a touch of citronelle and a nostalgic note of sun-ripened fruits. The range of perfumes produced by the rose is even more subtle than its palette of colors and is of an extraordinary richness, unequaled in any other flower. The work of the perfumer is to capture these precious fragrances and show them off to their best advantage.

Scented Roses

The rose has been universally used by perfumers ever since scent first existed, because it has four hundred volatile components to give it its inimitable depth. However, among the hundreds of types of rose, only two varieties are grown for their scent. *Rosa centifolia* is mainly grown in southern France, around the little town of Grasse, near Nice, which is the most famous perfumery center in the world. *Rosa centifolia* is the famous hundred-leaved or "May rose" and it is also grown in Morocco. The damask rose, *Rosa damascena*, is the most widely grown rose for perfumery, and is cultivated in Bulgaria, Turkey, and India. It produces the famous attar or otto of roses. The mixture of the two varieties is said to produce the most subtle rose perfume in the world. No essence is used in so many different perfumes as rose essence. These include the unique aroma of Cabochard by Grès and the cool purity of Anaïs Anaïs by Cacharel, the light gaiety of Fleurs de Rocaille by Caron and that of Trésor by Lancôme,

The famous damask or Damascus rose (Rosa damascena) is cultivated in Turkey and Bulgaria, growing into bushes the height of a man in fields that stretch as far as the horizon. There are wonderful depictions of the very ancient damask rose in eighteenth-century Persian miniatures. The exquisite, slightly musky odor has provided the headnotes for the most prestigious of French perfumes, such as Infini by Caron, Imprévu by Coty, Joy by Jean Patou, and Y by Yves Saint Laurent.

which has the fragrance of an Italian garden.

The number of rose growers around Grasse has decreased considerably in recent years, but the cultivation and picking, which require commitment and delicacy, are still very much part of the landscape. Although the Grasse essence is reputed to be too expensive, it has always been considered to be the most valuable and it is still the most sought-after. The extraordinary magnificence of the rose fields in May, their smooth, velvety perfume full of rich, subtle notes, is an unforgettable experience.

From Petals to Perfumes

An Arab legend tells how, in the tenth century, pilgrims returning from Mecca were struck with the perfume and beauty of the damask rose. They picked a few stems and replanted them when they returned to their homes in southern Morocco. Ever since, in the arid valley of Dadès, when May comes around and a faint breeze wafts over the tight rows of wild roses with their peppery scent, through the fields of barley and alfalfa at the approaches to Kelaa M'Gouna and Souk Khemis, there is the stunning sight

In its light petals, packed tightly into burlap sacks, the rose conceals the most complex perfume that exists, a perfume that can resemble that of violets, peaches, or lemon (above).

The famous May rose grown around Grasse, France, produces an essence which is of an unequaled beauty. One ton of petals, which must be hand-picked, produces 200 grams (about 7 ounces) of essence (overleaf).

of thousands of fresh flowers being gathered in woven baskets or in the long veils in which the women envelop themselves. The petals are deposited on the ground and are piled up in soft mattresses, which the men delicately turn over before hoisting them into copper vats where they will produce their rare attar from the tons of soft, sweet blooms. Once harvesting is complete, the rose festival is celebrated, bringing all the inhabitants of the region together wearing all their finery. The young girls, necks bowed with necklaces of flowers, throw handfuls of petals into the crowd while they dance and sing.

May is the month when the rose opens its petals in the countries where it is grown for its fragrance, and it is the time for the harvest in the mountain valleys of Bulgaria and Isparta, in Anatolia, Turkey. The air is impregnated with the sweet smell of roses. It wafts over the houses and their inhabitants, and even the horses smell of roses. There are vintages of Bulgarian and Turkish attar of roses, since the fragrance will vary depending on the year and the fields in which the bushes grew. It is one of the most valuable essences, a sort of liquid gold which gives depth to fragrances.

There is a romantic legend about how essence of roses came to be produced in India. It is set in the garden of the Mogul emperor Jahangir, at Shalimar. One day, Jahangir was sailing in his royal barge on a canal of rosewater, accompanied by one of his wives, Nur Jahan. She noticed that a foam was forming on the surface of the water. This was the intoxicating fragrance of the essential oil that was being distilled naturally through the action of the sun. Since then, the essence has been made in wooden casks which are subjected to the heat of the day and the cool of the night.

Today, the petals are subjected to various treatments in order to extract their quintessence and gain access to their secrets. Distillation consists in capturing the odoriferous compounds of the rose in water vapor by heating in a still. The rose petals need to be aerated in huge hangars before being packed into the distillation

In a dizzying rain of petals, centifolia roses are turned after harvesting in the Dades Valley in Morocco (facing page). The essence of roses is called "attar" in Turkish, hence the name attar or otto of roses for the raw material of perfumery. Attar from Isparta, in Anatolia, is sold in some of the stores in Istanbul (below). Roses are stored in a drying room at the firm of Giraudon-Roure, Grasse, where they wait to release their fragrances (bottom).

Distillation consists in capturing the odoriferous molecules in water vapor (steam) by placing the roses in an alambic or still (bottom). La Fête des Roses is a perfume that was launched by Caron in 1936 and sold in a crystal flask (below). Caron's boutique in Paris was opened in 1982 (facing page).

vats. A silky layer weighing 5 tons is needed to produce just over 2 pounds in weight (1 kilogram) of essential oil (also known as the essence). The petals are mixed with five times their weight in water and brought to the boil. The fragrance-laden steam rises through a narrow neck, and is then cooled to form droplets on the sides of the vat. The rosewater that condenses after the distillation process is used in cookery and cosmetics.

Enfleurage is another extraction technique, which exploits the ability of grease to absorb odors until it is saturated. The rose petals are steeped in vats of grease in which they release their perfume. The grease is then washed with alcohol to obtain the concrete, a heavily fragrant paste. Once the waxy element of the concrete has been removed, what remains is the absolute, the purest essence that leaves a strong impression on the nose. "Smelling of roses" is a very inaccurate expression. The absolute essential oil of French roses and the Bulgarian essences are actually as different as Bordeaux and Burgundy wines. The essence of the May rose, which is yellow-gold in color, has a honeyed, spicy smell, one that is less pronounced than that of the damask rose, whose color is orange-yellow. It is true that the perfume of an old-fashioned rose is more exquisite than any other floral perfume, and that you can immerse yourself in it without ever losing that sensation of sheer delight.

The Rose and Perfumers

Through transformation by the perfumer, roses have given their scents to a wide variety of perfumes. Some are peppery, others fruity, some are acidic, others smell of irises.

Fashion has in some respects eclipsed the single-stemmed rose, whose rather old-fashioned perfume is derived from a single species of flower. Today, such perfumes as Rose by Molinard (1860), Rose Jacqueminot by Coty (1904) and even Rose by d'Orsay (1908) are long forgotten, but anyone who likes pure rose perfume can

indulge themselves in London, where the famous perfumer Floris sells a brand called China Rose, a complex bouquet of exotic roses with an oriental sweetness, and Zinnia, a combination of roses, violets, and irises against a background woody notes. Another English firm, Crabtree and Evelyn, has created a perfume which they have called Evelyn, which is the perfect transcription of an old rose created by David Austin. Another of the famous English botanist's roses, "Abraham Darby," formed the basis of a scent created by Sylvie and Olivia Chantecaille in New York. Called Darby Rose, it is claimed to impart a sense of wellbeing and happiness.

Shakespeare described the rose's delicious perfume thus: "The rose looks fair, but fairer we it deem / For that sweet odour which doth in it live." Some nuances of rose fragrances are almost fruity, smelling of apricots or pineapples, but there is nothing like the "true" perfume of the rose. Several modern fragrances are based on the essence of roses. One of the most typical was created in 1976 by Houbigant and is called A Rose is a Rose, a quotation from the famous poem by Gertrude Stein. There is also Rose Absolue by Annick Goutal, which delicately combines the fragrances of Bulgarian and Turkish roses, May roses, and roses from Egypt and Morocco. Sonia Rykiel has produced her own rose perfume, whose pink bottle comes in a pink box. Rykiel Rose is a delicious alchemy of roses in which one can indulge with exquisite pleasure. Voleur de Roses (Rose Thief) by the firm of l'Artisan Parfumeur is a fragrance for men, and is based on notes designed to evoke green moss, damp earth, and rather peppery odors, while Drôle de Rose (A Funny Rose) is a very feminine creation with woody, fruity undertones.

The perfumer Jean-François Laporte has described the association of ideas which led him to concoct the eau de toilette he calls Rose Opulente: "A red rose on a long stem, half-opened on a fine morning in a garden under the rising sun…but the fragrance has only begun to make itself felt, though soon it is intoxicating, surprising in its roundness like the voluptuous feel of silk velvet…."

The rose sings solo in a number of contemporary fragrances, including Evelyn by Crabtree and Evelyn, Ce Soir ou Jamais (Tonight or Never) by Annick Goutal, China Rose by Floris (above), and 2000 and One Roses by Lancôme

For the salon in the Palais Royal, Paris, owned by the Japanese beauty products firm of Shiseido, the extraorindary perfurmer Serge Lutens created Rose de Nuit, which he describes as "an extreme perfume, which radiates to the maximum. It is a carpet of roses. The absolute of the Turkish rose gives the general color of the fragrance a rich and honeyed note." His new collection contains Sa Majesté la Rose, which bears the imprint of its creator, always the perfectionist. It is disturbing, elegant, and sensuous. Patricia de Nicolaï, a young perfumer who won the international prize for the best perfumer in 1989, created her own rose perfume which she called Jardin Secret (Secret Garden) and which expresses all the splendor of roses from the Atlas

Darby Rose (above left),
concocted by Sylvie and Olivia Chantecaille,
was inspired by "Abraham Darby,"
a variety created in 1985
by David Austin.
"Grand Siècle" (above right)
is "the rose par excellence,"
claims Henri Delbard:
"it gives me the inspiration to
discover other perfumes."
Rykiel Rose, Sonia Rykiel's
latest creation, continues
and amplifies the theme
of the rose (right).

Four superb homages to the rose: Rose de Nuit is an "extreme" perfume created by Serge Lutens, while Un Amour by Jean Patou is a gentle flower fragrance (below). There is the daring Poiray perfume in a bottle resembling a single bloom (right) and Féerie Rose by Patricia de Nicolaï, in its pink tissue paper wrappings (facing page). The unusual cup-shaped "Charles de Gaulle" rose combines rich mauve coloring with an intense perfume (bottom).

Mountains of Morocco, while Rose Pivoine (Peony Rose) is said to recall the morning dew in a garden filled with roses and peonies. She also makes bespoke perfumes for very rich, eccentric clients, such as a certain Japanese woman who is passionate about roses. "So I conjured up a rose perfume, which I called Féérie Rose. My client ordered three thousand Baccarat crystal bottles of the perfume, because she also wanted to give it as a gift to her friends."

Christine Nagel, the perfumer who created the perfume entitled 2000 et Une Roses for Lancôme, also paid homage to the queen of flowers in the perfume which she invented for the jeweler Poiray. It was a daring, spicy scent which spreads like a fragrant garden of wild briar roses, whose amber background notes are combined with sandalwood and vanilla.

Roses for Beautifying

As the flower of Venus and Aphrodite, beloved of Cleopatra and Nefertiti, the rose has been a beauty secret since Antiquity. Apart from its perfume, the rose encapsulates the magic power of beauty. When Elisabeth Vigée-Lebrun painted the portrait of Marie-Christine de Bourbon, seated elegantly beside a rosebush in her white muslin gown, she depicted her picking the flowers to lay them in her basket. This was to highlight her rosy complexion and the delicate tint of her cheeks.

Among Lancôme's range of cosmetics, the rose predominates. The firm's most popular lipstick is called Rose de France, though it is scented with Bulgarian attar of roses. Rouge, nail polish, and lipsticks all reflect the range of rose colors and hues, including pink, coral, golden rose, or amber rose. Bourjois uses rose chéri chéri, cendre de rose, venetian rose, and rose "vive la mariée" (bless the bride), while Estée Lauder draws on rose desire, apricot rose, and tea rose. The most recent collection of cosmetics from the eminent firm of Guerlain

Washing with rose-scented products gives an intense feeling of freshness and sensual delight. Below are a tea rose soap by Roger et Gallet, Rosa Magnifica by Guerlain, and Drôle de Rose by l'Artisan Parfumeur, with rose-petal-shaped soaps (bottom).

in Paris features a range called Rosa Spirit. It consists of a trio of beauty products entitled Rose Pomponnette combining a translucent powder, blusher, and lipstick.

Rosewater cleansing lotion is very easy to make at home, and even today it is considered to be an excellent astringent for improving the complexion. The recipe is simple: put about 2 ounces (40 grams) of fresh rose petals into a large bowl, then pour 1 pint (60 centiliters) of boiling water over them. Add a tablespoon of cider vinegar, cover and leave for two hours. Then filter the liquid into a very clean bottle or flask which should preferably be stored in the refrigerator (for up to three days).

If the rose flourishes as a perfume, it is also an important ingredient in creams and body lotions, gels and soaps, cleansers and skin care products. Once embalmed with these luxurious ointments, and steeped

in their fragrance, when you close your eyes, you get the impression that you are walking through a field of roses.

This is the illusion given by the tea-rose-scented anti-ageing cream created by Shiseido, the Fleur de Rocaille bath products by Caron, the stimulant concentrate by Decléor, composed of plant extracts and musk rose, or the natural beauty products, also scented with musk rose, created by the Weleda laboratories. In fact, their musk roses come from plants picked by hand high in the Andes during the Chilean fall, which lasts from February through May, when the rose hips are at their ripest. When applied to the skin, it leaves a delicate and subtle floral perfume.

This is how beauty products draw on the extraordinary riches of botany. The molecules extracted from the rose, whether astringent and stimulating, tranquilizing or protective, are a promise of radiant beauty. L'Eau Rose by Agnès B. thus provides a happy combination of the aromatic delights of the rose with the tonic freshness of a rehydrating eau de toilette.

Followers of a trend for natural products made from natural ingredients, two firms in Provence are famous for the outstanding quality of their cosmetics, and they are a good illustration of the reviving popularity of rose scents. Côté Bastide produces perfumed eaux de toilette and bath oils, soaps, bath salts and essences, foam baths and flower waters, all of them delicately perfumed with old-fashioned roses. The products are packaged in thick white paper with the name of the contents beautifully inscribed in black ink in a copperplate script. The garden collection of L'Occitane contains several perfumes associated with various scents. Those which bear the name Neroli Rose combine the orange-blossom freshness of neroli and petitgrain with the superb fragrance of the rose, together with jasmine, muguet, iris and peach. This fragrance is produced as an eau de toilette, an extract and a concrete, a shower gel, a bath and a perfumed lotion.

Delicate and smelling of irises, intense and fruity or opulent and cloying, the fragrance of the rose always evokes beauty, luxury, and elegance. Fragonard illustrates these qualities with its foam bath, soap, and shower splash (below); and Côté Bastide with its flower waters and bath salts (bottom).

On the skin and in the hair, as a perfume and throughout the house, the delicious rose makes its presence felt. There are special fragrances for perfuming a room (below, Rose des Indes by Jean-François Laporte) as well as rose-scented linen water for sprinkling while ironing, by L'Occitane (bottom), so that the rose fragrance can pervade the linen closet. In order to prolong the effect of these long lasting fragrances, one need merely light a rose-scented candle, or create potpourris with garden fragrances (facing page).

Perfumes for the Home

Bouquets of fresh roses are undoubtedly the most exquisite of natural fragrances with which to perfume an interior. In order to add to or extend the effect of these scents, specialist florists Au Nom de la Rose have created an entire fragrant environment dedicated to the rose. Molinard created a delicate Eau de Rose (rosewater) for the store, as well as rose-scented beads for perfuming linen, perfumed candles, and soaps shaped like petals.

L'Occitane draws its inspiration from the wonderful scents of the wildflowers of Provence and has created a range of special mixtures for the home that are spicy, flowery, and fruity, and which are produced in the form of candles, vaporizing fragrances and incense cones, powders to be sprinkled before vacuuming, potpourris and plant amber. Rose-lovers will naturally choose Rose Poivre, a successful combination of a crimson rose with a sophisticated fragrance and a fruity, peppery note, smoothed with vanilla and apricot.

In Morocco, rosewater is sprinkled as a symbol of hospitality and purification. It is the custom to do so on religious festivals and when entertaining guests on formal occasions. A generous libation, it is a sign of welcome, and at banquets the diners are sprinkled with rosewater from long-necked flasks with silvered metal caps. Rose petals may be scattered on the table or the ground, while rosewater refreshes and perfumes the clothing. The Berber rose is a talisman and good luck charm which protects the wearer against the evil eye. When Saladin recaptured Jerusalem from the Crusaders in 1187, he ordered the Mosque of Omar (the Dome of the Rock), which had been converted into a church by the Christians, to be purified with rosewater brought from Damascus in a caravan of five hundred camels.

On a humbler scale, l'Occitane has had the novel idea of creating a special rose perfume for sprinkling on linen while it is being ironed, so that the scent can pervade bedroom and linen closets. It can also be poured into a steam iron and used instead of distilled water. Au Nom de la Rose tries to create the same effect with rose-scented pearls to be slipped among the linen.

Fragrant roses have the magic power to retain their perfume long after their petals have faded. That is why the world of roses is also that of potpourri, a custom originating from England which is said to date from the Elizabethan era. Gertrude Jekyll, the famous landscape gardener who lived and worked in the late nineteenth and early twentieth centuries, discusses in great detail how she made her own potpourri. Over a period lasting several months, she would pick bushels of rose petals early in the morning, once the dew had evaporated. She would leave them to dry spread out in a thin layer on a cloth in a cool, dry place, then she would put them in jars and sprinkle them with salt. Geranium (pelargonium) leaves, lavender flowers, and bitter orange peel were preserved in the same way. On a bright sunny day in late summer, everything would be poured out of the jars onto the brick paving of the terrace. Friends and children were rounded up and came to help mix the ingredients. Additional items were added, including mace, cloves, allspice, benzoin, and an orris root concoction called Atkinson's violet powder. Armed with pokers and small spades, the potpourri-makers stirred and turned the large pile so that at the end of the day, all that there remained to do was to pour it all into a big wooden barrel.

The sweet, light fragrance of rose-scented potpourri cannot fail to be reminiscent of rose bowers and old-fashioned cottage gardens, and adds a special atmosphere to any home, whether in the countryside or the heart of the city. Among the dozens of modern recipes for potpourri, this one is based on ingredients that are already dried, and is quick and easy to create. Mix 6 ounces (150 grams) of dried scented red rose petals, 2 ounces (50 grams) of rose petals, 2 ounces of camomile flowers, 2 ounces of small pieces of cassia bark, 2 ounces of orris root, and 1 ounce (30 grams) of pieces of oak-moss; add 20 drops of essential oil of roses, mix again, and pour it all into an attractive shallow bowl.

Roses for the Gourmet

*It was as if a strange alchemical process had dissolved
her entire being in the rose petal sauce, in the tender
flesh of the quails, in the wine, in every one of the meal's
aromas. That was the way she entered Pablo's body;
hot, voluptuous, perfumed, totally sensuous.*

Laura Esquivel, Like Water for Chocolate

*Master confectioners
are able to imitate in
sugar the infinite delicacy
of rose petals wrapped
around a corolla
(right).*

hen a man presents his sweetheart with the gift of a dozen roses, he hardly expects her to make them into a salad or a sauce! Yet flowers in general, and roses in particular, have always played an important role as a luxury food throughout Europe and the Middle and Far East. The use of roses in cuisine has a long history. The Chinese were probably the first to popularize the rose as food. Travelers' tales recount how in Nanking, the capital of China during the Middle Ages, there was an intensive rose-growing industry to produce petals to be used to flavor tea and pastries, as well as a liqueur called "sand of roses."

Banquets of Roses

t the banquets of ancient Rome, the tables and food were covered in rose petals, and the stores of the *rosarii*, the florists who specialized in roses, were as popular as those of the butchers and bakers. Roses were made into garlands and wound around goblets for the purpose of a toast called "drinking the wreaths." The petals were scattered into the wine and were imbibed with the liquid. The Romans also loved a type of alcoholic drink obtained by macerating roses and other plants in must. They also made a sauce called *rosatum*, created by macerating fresh rose petals, renewed three times a day for seven days, to which honey was added. This was used to flavor fish or game stews with an extravagant richness of flavors. Pliny the Elder tells how "a number of elegant dishes arrived on the table, sprinkled with rose petals or soaked in their liquid which does absolutely no harm to meats and gives them a good flavor."

Syrups and Confectionery

resh, dried, crystallized, candied, or macerated, rose petals have featured since time immemorial among the list of ingredients used in medieval and Oriental cuisine. Nearer our own time, Bartolomeo Stefani, the

Thanks to its beauty, coloring, and fragrance, the rose long ago made its entrance into the delicious realm of gourmet foods. It can be made into a scarlet syrup with ruby highlights (page 137) and petals of every shade can be candied in confectioner's sugar (pages 137 and facing). Miniature dried rosebuds (below) are used in Indian, Chinese, and Moroccan cooking, to make fruit teas and infusions, and are also added to spice mixtures which are added to such foods as duck terrine.

It is extremely easy to make rose-flavored tea. Just mix 8 ounces (250 grams) of China or Indian tea with 3½ ounces (100 grams) of strongly perfumed dried rose petals (bottom). Delicious rose-flavored syrups are made in Cyprus, Tunisia, Morocco, India, and Pakistan (below). In Paris, the firm of Goumanyat makes a rose and hibiscus liqueur (facing page). It is an ingredient in cocktails, but can also be used as a sauce for fresh fruits, sweetened with acacia honey.

official chef at the court of the Gonzagas, in a book published in 1662, offers a recipe for preserving whole roses. The roses are washed and dipped in bunches of three into a sugar syrup where they must remain for about ten minutes. "They are then placed in little cups in such a way that no flower must touch another. Return the syrup to the heat and when it is well cooked, pour it over the roses; for banquets, one or two could be served to each diner, coated with a syrup of jasmine flowers."

The rose in cookery is not merely the preserve of weird and wonderful Roman orgies or obscure medieval preparations. It continues to flavor foods to this day.

A trip to Istanbul is an opportunity to sample such Turkish delicacies as rose preserves and rose jelly, in order to understand how the rose can be converted into a divine food, the color of a jewel, with the consistency of honey. The great classic of all oriental delicacies is, of course, Turkish delight, known in Turkey and the Arab world as *rahat loukoum,* the classic oriental candy, which tastes like something out of the Arabian Nights. Even the name itself, which means "the relaxation of the throat," is romantic. In the darkened interior of a traditional confectioner's store in the market in the old neighborhood of Galatasaray, in Istanbul, these little opalescent cubes, lightly dusted with powdered sugar, melt in the mouth with a delicious rose perfume of incredible sweetness.

Rosewater and essence of roses have traditionally been used to give a delicate aroma to flower liqueurs and wines, creams, ices, and desserts of all types, such as the traditional Turkish and Arab cold rice pudding called *muhallabieh* generously flavored with rosewater, which tastes so exquisitely fresh on the tongue. Dried, powdered rosebuds are also used as a spice, either alone or with other ingredients. They are included in the spice mix used in so many North African dishes called *ras el-hanout* (meaning "head of the store"). The mixture varies but generally includes cinnamon, cloves, and *shoosh al-ward* (dried musk-rose buds). The ingredients are crushed to a powder in a mortar and mixed well.

One might also succumb to the temptation of

When one has a weakness for sweets, melting Turkish delights are an incomparable pleasure. These little opalescent cubes sprinkled with powdered sugar, as luminous as jewels, are perfumed with rosewater (top). Christine Ferber is a French confectioner who pleases the most demanding gourmets with her confections. Her rose-petal jam and her raspberry jelly with rose petals are among the most delectable of delights (above).

tasting crunchy, fried whole rosebuds. This most romantic of dishes is a Moroccan invention.

In Turkey and in North Africa, chicken dishes are often flavored with roses, sometimes with jasmine. The Moroccans produce a most exquisite preserve, a spiced mixture of tomatoes candied in honey and mixed with Dadès roses, which is used as a condiment to eat with a variety of game or lamb dishes.

Confectioners are also well aware of the irresistible attraction of the rose, its color and fragrance. It is difficult not to succumb to the temptation of such delicacies as apple jelly with rose petals or petal jam, which the firm of Hédiard markets alongside other rose specialties, such as rose syrup and rose-scented tea. The pleasure of buying a bouquet of real roses at Au Nom de la Rose, the Parisian florist, could well be extended by a purchase of rose preserves for spreading on toast at an elegant tea party, or a rose-flavored syrup to sweeten a glass of champagne. Macaroons are another specialty of the French capital. The firm of Ladurée has always been famous for this crunchy little cookie with a soft interior, and the most delicious is the rose-flavored macaroon which seems to contain the very heart of the rose. Fauchon, the most famous of the Parisian gourmet food stores, has created a confection which it calls *Le Paradis* (Paradise) consisting of a froth of rose petals hidden inside a sponge cake (an old-fashioned specialty), as well as a gourmet pyramid of rose-flavored macaroons. The Goumanyat confectionery store sells rose comfits and candied rose petals which are a delight to the eyes as well as well as to the tastebuds. And the *chocolatier* Richart has created a ganache cream filling flavored with verbena leaves and rose petals.

The tradition of edible roses in France owes much to Thibaud de Champagne, who returned from the Crusades in the thirteenth century, bringing with him a strongly aromatic red rose which became almost a cult object. The dried petals of the rose de Provins were exported all over Europe to flavor the most varied foods. A local confectioner continues to make the famous rose-petal jelly which in French is called *confit de roses de Provins*, thus perpetuating the tradition in the little town of Provins in the Brie region. The recipe requires the roses to be picked in mid-September. They must be fully open crimson roses and the petals are sorted, washed, and cooked in boiling water.

Garden Roses in the Kitchen

A question immediately arises concerning the use of roses in cookery. Which types of rose should be chosen? The connoisseurs are unanimous on this point. The best roses for use in cookery are from the garden, preferably dark-colored (red or dark pink) and of the old-fashioned type (which retain their color for quite a long time,) and, of course, heavily scented. *Rosa gallica*, the

The famous rose preserve, a specialty shared historically by the Turks and the French city of Provins, is a particularly delicious teatime treat, spread on toast or warm brioche. It should be served in a suitably attractive pot, matching its refinement, delicate flavor, and smooth texture.

The petals of scented roses destined for cooking must be picked in the early morning. The white part of the petal, at the calyx end, which is a little tough, should be cut away and discarded (bottom). The petals can then be crystallized, that is, dipped in egg white, sprinkled with powdered sugar, and dried completely. When carefully arranged on an elegant dessert they are an irresistible invitation to indulge (below).

damask rose, the moss rose or the centifolia all give excellent results. They must be picked early in the morning and must be fully opened, and fragrant. The gourmets will tell you that roses bought from the florist for this purpose will always disappoint. But take, for example, the wild rose, *Rosa rugosa*, which is deep red, pink, or white. It has an exquisite scent and is as delicious to eat as it is to smell.

As for the cultivated roses, the varieties developed by David Austin, especially "Gertrude Jekyll" and "Constance Spry," are highly recommended. Many others are also delicious. These include "Tiffany," "New Dawn," and "Charles de Mills," as well as "Papa Meilland" and "Madame Isaac Pereire." The ideal moment to pick the petals is early on a warm, sunny morning in July or August. Before using the petals, the white part at the base must be trimmed away, as it tastes bitter. The best way to do this is to hold all the petals of a rose in one hand and expose the white part by twisting them. Then clip out the white part with a pair of scissors held in the other hand. Spread out the petals on a clean cloth, brushing away any insects with a fine brush.

Alice Caron Lambert, a world expert in floral flavors, and the author of more than four hundred recipes based on edible flowers, has performed research into flavors based on eighty-seven rose scents, twenty-five types of rose hip, and two types of rose leaf. "There are fruity, peppery, musky, floral, woody, lemony, spicy, and amber scents," she explains, "all of which taste delicious in cookery."

Rose-Flavored Desserts

Clearly the rose predominates in all types of sweet dishes, including desserts and candies. Pierre Hermé, who was chief confectioner to the firm of Fauchon, wrote a book entitled *Secrets gourmands* (Gourmet Secrets) in which he published the recipe for rose-petal ice cream, which uses five untreated "Sonia" roses. The flowers are stripped of their leaves and the petals trimmed as

described above, then plunged into a boiling mixture of milk and light cream. They are left to infuse for fifteen minutes, then strained, pressing down hard on the petals. This creamy, scented milk is allowed to cool slightly, and then rose syrup and rosewater are added to it. Egg yolks and sugar are beaten vigorously, and the rose mixture added to them. This is then cooked to just below boiling point like a custard. It is left to cool, then frozen and served as it is or accompanied by a raspberry sorbet or caramel-flavored ice cream. It is also possible to make rose-petal sorbet by mixing hot sugar syrup and strongly scented dark red roses.

Syllabub is a traditional English dessert which dates back at least to the time of Elizabeth I. It consists of whipped cream (originally milk straight from the cow's udder into the mixing bowl!), sweet white wine, lemon

Dark red, heavily scented roses are best suited for culinary purposes. "Papa Meilland," a magnificent dark red rose, with velvety petals, created in 1963, is excellent for the purpose. It has an exceptionally strong, almost intoxicating, fragrance, whose notes are both rosy and lemony. This is a hardy variety that does well in any garden and flowers abundantly.

Au Nom de la Rose was the first florist in modern times in Europe to sell nothing but roses, and everything connected therewith. It has turned this flower into a lifestyle, selling fragrances and decorative items, as well as gourmet foods such as this rose-petal jam with its golden glints (above). This soft, round cookie is the trademark of the firm of Ladurée. It is a rose-flavored macaroon, whose flavor and fragrance are quite distinctive. It was the result of a quest for a light pastel coloring and a smoother flavor redolent of trips to the Orient. Its flower-scented fragrance and melting texture blend perfectly with its flavor and color (facing page).

juice, and sugar. When rose flavoring is added this gives it an even more delicious flavor.

To serve four people, finely grate the zest from two untreated lemons and macerate it in a glass of sweet sherry, adding three tablespoons of sugar and the juice of one lemon. Mix this preparation with 8 fluid ounces (1 cup / 250 milliliters) of crème fraîche or heavy cream, the juice of the other lemon, and a few drops of essence of rose. Whip the mixture until it thickens, then divide the syllabub between frosted sundae glasses, and sprinkle with crystallized rose petals.

According to a traditional Turkish recipe for rose-petal preserves, the fragrant petals of *Rosa centifolia* should be picked early in the morning, while still covered in dew, then the white part, where the petal is attached to the calyx, must be discarded, as it is slightly tough and bitter. The petals are then boiled in an equal weight of petals, sugar, and water. The mixture is left to thicken on a low heat until it reaches a syrupy consistency, then a squirt of lemon juice is added. This delicious preserve is often served in Turkey and in Bulgaria with farmer or cream cheese, or with vanilla ice cream.

The rose features prominently in Indian cuisine, especially in the Baltistan region, in the heart of the Himalayas. Dried rose petals are incorporated into the spice mixture known as *garam masala*, which flavors meat or poultry. The raw petals are added to salads, and essence of rose perfumes milk puddings. Rose petals are added to the water in finger bowls at elegant dinners.

For those who love roses in all their forms, there are a few very simple recipes which can be used so that the flavor and scent of roses can be enjoyed daily, in tea or in sugar. The most suitable tea for scenting with a rose fragrance is the China tea variety known as Oolong, which is amber in color and has a slightly fruity odor. Mix 8 ounces (2 cups / 250 grams) of tea leaves with 3 ½ ounzes (⅔ cup / 100 grams) of strongly scented, dried rose petals, and store the mixture in a hermetically sealed metal tin.

To make rose sugar, the proportions are 8 ounces (2cups / 250 grams) of powdered (confectioner's) sugar for ¾ ounce

(3 tablespoons / 20 grams) of coarsely ground dried petals. Rose sugar is delicious when added to the pastry for fruit tarts, to sprinkle on plain yogurt, or on pot or farmer cheese.

Rose Drinks

Using roses from your own garden, you can make a refreshing drink from an ancient recipe, whose flavor is like a poem. Simply take a large handful of brightly colored, well-perfumed petals. Pour some spring water into a pot, add the petals, and boil for one minute. Remove from the heat, cover, and leave to infuse the whole night. The next day, add the juice of a lemon, mix and filter, sweeten with sugar or honey, and serve with crushed ice in tall glasses, floating a few fresh petals on the surface.

Rose liqueur is quite easy to make, but you must choose fully open and strongly scented roses. After washing and drying them on a clean cloth, detach the petals. Take a large, wide-mouthed preserving jar and pour a layer of petals into the bottom, then cover with a layer of superfine sugar. Repeat the alternate layers of petals and sugar (two volumes of petals for one volume of sugar), until the jar is full. Close the jar and leave it for a week, then add 16 fluid ounces (2 cups / 1 liter) of 40° liquor or vodka, close it again, and leave for another week. Filter the liquid and bottle it.

A rose punch is a deliciously refreshing and perfumed summer drink. In a large bowl, leave 1¼ pounds (4 cups / 500 grams) of rose petals to macerate with 3½ ounces (¾ cup / 100 grams) of sugar and a small glass of raspberry liqueur. Cover and leave for one hour, then add a bottle of dry white wine and leave for another hour. Strain the liquid into a punch bowl, add the contents of a chilled bottle of champagne and plenty of ice, and serve.

There is an even more subtle rose-flavored liqueur, the exquisite elixir of roses made in Florence, Italy, by the Officina Profumo-Farmaceutica Santa Maria Novella. Fresh rose petals are macerated in very pure alcohol. The mixture

Elixir of roses is produced and bottled by the Officina Profumo-Farmaceutica Santa Maria Novella in Florence, Italy, one of the oldest pharmacies in the world. It is a liqueur obtained by a secret process whereby fresh rose petals are macerated in very pure alcohol. It is tonic and has an exquisite flavor (facing page). If rosewater is used to flavor cakes, cookies, and desserts, this wine from Provence, produced on the hills of Gassin, is called Pétale de rose due to its elegant color. It is a classic rosé, vinified in the traditional way (below).

It took American pastry chef Ann Amernick long hours to shape, paint, and assemble the pulled-sugar petals of this wedding cake (facing page). Pastillage is another technique used by confectioners. A mixture of powdered sugar, corn-starch, and gelatin is kneaded to a malleable consistency so that it can be modeled like clay into the most realistic sculptures (bottom, pastillage roses by Lenôtre). These candied roses are easier to make but just as decorative (below).

is said to have a revitalizing effect for convalescents. One has the feeling of absorbing, alongside the roses all the reinvigorating fragrances of a scented garden. "I remember sitting with Ambroise one evening, as in the groves of Academe. We sat ourselves on an ancient tomb, completely surrounded by cypresses; we chatted at a leisurely pace, while chewing on rose petals…" wrote André Gide in *Nourritures Terrestres*.

Sugar Roses

The shape of the rose is so graceful that its use in decorating food is almost unavoidable. When picked just as it opens, a rose can be preserved for several months by being encrusted with sugar.

Real crystallized roses are an elegant and unusual decoration for desserts. Choose garden roses, preferably ones that are brightly colored and open, but not overblown. The blooms should be completely unblemished and, of course, free of any chemical treatment. Each petal should be entirely coated with a fine, even layer of lightly beaten egg white. This should be done with a soft, fine paintbrush. The rose is then sprinkled with an even layer of sifted confectioner's sugar and placed on a cake rack or other type of fine-meshed grille to dry in a cool, dry place.

Pulled sugar, sometimes called sugarcraft, is a unique material that experienced and skilled confectioners use to create amazing floral compositions of extraordinary realism. To make pulled sugar, cook a sugar syrup to the hard crack stage, pour it onto a marble work surface and add a few drops of coloring. Then work it and pull it while it is warm and malleable until it turns shiny, then mold it into the desired shape. Sugar roses made in this way can be pale and creamy, fully opened into silky blooms. They are assembled petal by petal into wreaths and bouquets and used to decorate tiered wedding cakes. The recent fashion for rolled glacé frosting to decorate cakes, so that the frosting does not have the hard, sharp, powdery edge of royal icing, lends itself particularly well to rose decorations.

Useful Addresses

ROSE GARDENS OPEN TO THE PUBLIC

The choice of rose gardens open to the public, both in the U.S. and Europe, is immense. At the following addresses you are guaranteed a magnificent spectacle of roses, both ancient and modern, between the months of May and September.

United States

Morcom Amphitheater of Roses
700 Jean Street,
Oakland, CA 94612
Tel.: (510) 238-3187
The garden provides an opportunity to view over 500 rose species, including a collection of historic hybrid teas from the 1920s to the 1950s.

Arboretum of Los Angeles County
301 North Baldwin Avenue,
Arcadia, CA 91007-2697
Tel.: (626) 821-3222
This garden includes a fascinating collection of Shakespeare's herbs.

Berkeley Rose Garden
Department of Parks
1201 Euclid Ave,
Berkeley, CA 94708
Tel.: (415) 644-6530
One of the highlights of this garden is the rose amphitheater with tiers of different-colored roses descending to the base.

Elizabeth Park Rose Garden
150, Walbridge Road,
West Hartford, CT 06119
Tel.: (860) 242-0017
This exceptional garden has some 800 varieties of rose, in addition to one-hundred-year-old greenhouses.

Longue Vue Gardens
7 Bamboo Road, New Orleans,
LA 70124-1065
Tel.: (504) 488-5488
Inspired by the fourteenth-century Generalife Gardens of the Alhambra in Spain.

William Paca Garden
1 Martin Street,
Annapolis, MD 21401
Tel.: (410) 267-6656
This site offers a stunning design for a small historic American-style town garden.

Hampton National Historic Site
535 Hampton Lane,
Towson, MD 21286
Tel.: (410) 962-0688
Large eighteenth-century Georgian mansion with extensive grounds including formal Italianate and English landscapes gardens.

Governor Langdon Mansion Memorial
143 Pleasant Street,
Portsmouth, NH 03801
Tel.: (603) 436-3205
This quiet refuge in the middle of town includes a formal perennial garden, rose arbor, and pinetum.

Rundlet-May House
364 Middle Street, Portsmouth,
NH 03801
Tel.: (603) 436-3205
The garden remains as laid out by James Rundlet in 1807 and includes formal terraces, as well as remnants of Rundlet's orchard.

Clark Botanic Garden
193 I. U. Willets Road, Albertson,
NY 11507
Tel.: (516) 484-8600
This twelve acre garden contains a range of shrubs, small trees, annuals, perennials and roses.

New York Botanical Garden
200th Street and Kazimiroff Street,
Bronx, New York,
NY 10458
Tel.: (718) 817-8700
Fax: (718) 817-8596
Community garden in the heart of the Bronx.

Dumbarton Oaks
1703 32nd Street NW,
Washington, DC 20007
Tel.: (202) 339-6410
This garden in Georgetown has a wide variety of plants and features. Its 25 planted terraces include a spectacular rose garden.

National Herb Garden,
U.S. National Arboretum
3501 New York Avenue NE,
Washington, DC 20002
Tel.: (202) 472-9259
This fascinating historic rose garden also has themed beds: dye, early American, medicine, oriental, culinary, Native American and others.

Washington National Cathedral Gardens
Wisconsin & Massachusetts Avenues NW,
Washington, DC 20016-5098
Tel.: (202) 537-2937
The 59-acre grounds of the cathedral include the Bishop's Garden, which is modeled on a medieval walled garden and contains a rose garden.

Canada

Centennial Rose Garden
Dogwood Pavilion,
621 Poirier St., Coquitlam BC
This beautiful garden contains over 900 hybrid teas and floribundas.

Jardin Botanique de Montréal
4101 Sherbrooke St. E.
Montreal,
Quebec H1X 2B2
Tel.: (514) 872-1400
www.ville-montreal.qc.ca/jardin/
This is the largest rose garden in Canada, with in excess of 10,000 rosebushes.

Royal Botanical Gardens
680 Plains Road West,
Burlington, Ontario
www.rbg.ca
Many different types of roses, with a particular emphasis on miniatures.

Australia

Australian National Botanic Gardens
GPO Box 1777,
Canberra, ACT 2601
Tel.: 02-62509450
The Australian National Gardens play host to a range of roses as well as fascinating native species.

France

Hôtel Baudy,
Musée-Restaurant
81, rue Claude Monet,
27620 Giverny
Tel.: 02 32 21 10 03
A beautiful old-fashioned rose
garden in Claude Monet's village.

Roseraie du Val-de-Marne
8, rue Albert Watel,
94240 L'Haÿ-les-Roses
Tel.: 01 43 99 82 80
National conservatory for old-
fashioned roses, with 3,500
different varieties.

Germany

Europa-Rosarium
Steinberger Weg 3,
06526 Sangerhausen
Tel.: (03464) 57 25 22
www.europa-rosarium.de
A glorious state collection of
ancient roses.

Great Britain

Elsing Hall
Dereham, Norfolk
Tel.: (01362) 637224
Magnificent fifteenth-century
English manor, where two
dedicated rose enthusiasts,
David and Shirley Cargill, have
created a sumptuous collection
(largely based on Peter Beales'
creations) in the heart of the
English countryside.

**Garden of the Royal National
Rose Society**
Chiswell Green Lane,
Saint Albans, Herts AL2 3NR
Tel.: (01727) 850461
Each year, over thirty thousand
ancient and modern roses
provide a fine display
(accompanied by concerts and
plays).

Mottisfont Abbey Garden
Romsey, Hampshire S051 0LJ
Tel.: (01794) 340757
A jewel in the National Trust's
crown, with over 300 varieties of
old-fashioned roses in a delightful
setting.

Royal Botanic Gardens, Kew
Richmond, Surrey TW9 3AVB
Tel.: (0208) 940 1171
The extensive rose garden at Kew
contains 54 rose beds
displaying floribunda, hybrid tea,
and old English roses, all
arranged according to color.

Sissinghurst Castle,
Sissinghurst, Cranbrook,
Kent TN17 2AB
Tel.: (01580) 710701
The former residence of the famous
garden writer Vita Sackville-West,
practically unchanged since her time.

Sudeley Castle
Winchcombe, Cheltenham,
Gloucestershire GL54 5JD
Tel.: (01242) 602308
Victorian-style rose beds.

Italy

**Collection of Professor Fineschi
Cavriglia,**
San Giovanni Valdarno, Italy
Tel.: 055 966797
Said to be the world's largest
private collection, with 6,000
different species collected by a
true devotee, from the most old-
fashioned roses to the most
modern hybrids.

ROSE GROWERS AND NURSERIES

*The following addresses are particularly
recommended should you wish to start
growing your own roses.*

United States

Antique Rose Emporium
Rte 5, P.O. Box 143,
Brenham, TX 77833
Tel.: (409) 836-9051

Blossoms and Bloomers
E 11415 Krueger Lane
Spokane, WA 99207
Tel.: (509) 922-1344

Chamblee's Roses
10926 U.S. Hwy, 69 North
Tyler, TX 75706-8742
Tel.: (903) 882-3597
Email: roses@tyler.net
www.chambleeroses.com

Heirloom Roses
24062 NE Riverside Drive,
St. Paul, OR 97137
Tel.: (503) 538-1576
www.heirloomroses.com

Historical Roses
1657 West Jackson Street
Painesville, OH 44077
Tel.: (440) 357-7270

Mendocino Heirloom Roses
P.O. Box 670, Mendocino,
CA 95460
Tel.: (707) 937-0963
www.heritageroses.com

Muncy's Rose Emporium
11207 Celestine Pass,
Sarasota, FL 34240
Tel.: (941) 377-6156
Email:MuncyRose@flsuncoast.com

Canada

Hardy Roses for the North
P.O. Box 2048, Grand Forks,
BC V0H 1H0
Tel.: (604) 442-8442
Fax: (604) 442-2766

Mockingbird Lane Roses
4464 Clarke Road,
Port Burwell, Ontario N0J 1TO
Tel.: (519) 874-4811
www.mockingbird-lane.com

France

Delbard
16 quai de la Mégisserie,
75054 Paris cedex 01
Tel.: 01 44 88 80 00
Fax: 01 44 88 80 16

Meilland Richardier
50, rue Deperet,
69160 Tassin La Demi-Lune
Tel.: 04 78 34 46 52
Fax: 04 72 38 09 97
www.roses-fr.com

Roseraie de Berty
07110 Largentière
Tel.: 04 75 88 30 56

Les Roses Anciennes
d'André Eve
Morailles, B.P. 206
45302 Pithiviers-le-Vieil
Tel.: 02 38 30 01 30
Fax: 02 38 30 71 65

Great Britain

David Austin
Bowling Green Lane, Albrighton,
Wolverhampton WV7 3HB
Tel.: (01902) 37391

Peter Beales Roses
London Road, Attleborough,
Norfolk NR17 1AY
Tel.: (01953) 454707
Fax: (01953) 457145
www.classicroses.co.uk

R. Harkness & Co. Ltd.
Cambridge Road,
Hitchin, Herts SG4 OJT
Tel.: (01462) 420402
Email: harkness@roses.co.uk

**Trevor White Old-Fashioned
Roses**
Bennetts Brier, The Street,
Felthorpe, Norfolk NR10 4AB
Tel.: (01603) 755135

Buying your rosebushes on the internet:
www.plantes-et-jardins.com
www.markw.com/mailorder.htm

EXHIBITIONS AND
SHOWS

*Rose-lovers can visit a whole range of
events dedicated to the rose, all over
Europe and North America, from May
through September.*

Mid-May
Chelsea Flower Show
Royal Horticultural Society,
Royal Hospital, London SW3
Bookings: (0870) 906 3781

June
Festival des Roses
Jardins de Bagatelle, Paris
Tel.: 01 40 71 75 23

Canadian National Rose Show
Southshore Community Centre

Barrie, Ontario
Contact the Canadian Rose Society
for details (see below).

July
Rose Festival (early July)
Chiswell Green Lane,
Saint Albans, Hertfordshire

**City of Belfast International
Rose Trials**
Belfast, Northern Ireland
Tel.: (01232) 320202

**Hampton Court Palace Flower
Show and British Rose Festival**
(mid-July)
Royal Horticultural Society, London
Tel.: (0207) 649 1885

August
Glasgow Rose Trials (25th August)
Tel.: (0141) 287 5920

September
**American Rose Society
Convention**
Cleveland, Ohio
12th through 16th September
Contact the society for details (see
below).

For further details, contact:

AMERICAN ROSE SOCIETY
P.O. Box 30,000, Shreveport,
LA 71130-0030
Tel.: (318) 938-5402
Fax: (318) 938-5405
Email: ars@ars-hq.org
www.ars.org
Contact: Michael Kromer

HERITAGE ROSE FOUNDATION
1512 Gorman St., Raleigh,
NC 27606
Tel.: (919) 834-2591
Email: rosefoun@aol.com

CANADIAN ROSE SOCIETY
10, Fairfax Crescent
Scarborough, Ontario M1L 1Z8
Tel.: (416) 757-8809
Fax: (416) 757-4796
www.mirror.org/group/crs
Contact: Anne Graber

**ROYAL NATIONAL ROSE SOCIETY
(UK)**
The Gardens of the Rose,

Chiswell Green, Saint Albans,
Herts AL2 3NR
Tel.: (01727) 850461
Email: mail@rnrs.org.uk
www.roses.co.uk

**NATIONAL ROSE SOCIETY OF
AUSTRALIA**
271 b Belmore Road,
North Balwyn, Victoria 3104
Tel.: (3) 9857 9656
Contact: James Priestly

FLORISTS

*It is, of course, impossible to list all the
best florists, or even the best rose
specialists. However, here is a selection of
florists whose work in this book might
have inspired you.*

Au Nom de la Rose
(see pages 68, 72)
4, rue de Tournon,
75006 Paris
Tel.: 01 42 22 22 12

Baptiste (see page 64)
85, rue Vaneau,
75007 Paris
Tel.: 01 42 22 82 31

Stéphane Chapelle (see page 70)
29 rue de Richelieu,
75001 Paris
Tel.: 01 42 60 65 66

Comme à la Campagne
(see pages 57, 73)
29, rue du Roi de Sicile,
75004 Paris
Tel.: 01 40 29 09 90

Comme une Fleur
(see pages 74, 75)
55, rue de Lancry,
75010 Paris
Tel.: 01 44 05 20 16

Céline Dussaule
(see page 67)
10 rue Saint-Sabin,
75010 Paris
Tel.: 01 49 23 09 32

Didier-Pierre (see page 58)
114, boulevard Gallieni,
92130 Issy-les-Moulineaux
Tel.: 01 46 32 43 00

Les Milles Feuilles (see page 76)
2, rue Rambuteau,
75003 Paris
Tel.: 01 42 78 32 93

Marcel Wolterinck (see page 57)
Naarderstraat 13,
1251 AW Laren, Netherlands
Tel.: 35 53 83 909

Moulié (see page 55)
8, place du Palais-Bourbon,
75007 Paris
Tel.: 01 45 51 78 43

Christian Tortu (see page 73)
6, carrefour de l'Odéon,
75006 Paris
Tel.: 01 43 26 02 56

Rosa Rosa
141 E, 44th Street,
New York, NY 10017
Tel.: (212) 681-9770

Roses Only
1040, Avenue of the Americas,
New York, NY 10018
Tel.: (212) 869-7673

Internet florists and rose delivery:

www.800florals.com
www.interflora.com
www.universalflower.com
www.usaflower.com
www.justflowers.com
www.sayitwith.co.uk
www.fowlersfreshflowers.co.uk

DECORATION

The rose and decoration for the home have always gone hand in hand.

France

Au Fil des Couleurs
31, rue de l'Abbé Grégoire,
75006 Paris
Tel.: 01 45 44 74 00
Fax: 01 45 44 74 50
Madame Texier creates unique rose-patterned wallpapers on demand for her clients, including the beautiful old Mauny designs (see pages 105, 106).

Michèle Aragon
21, rue Jacob,
75006 Paris
Tel.: 01 43 25 87 69
This shop offers a vast choice of traditional *boutis* (Provençal prints) with floral motifs (see page 87).

Casa Lopez
39-41, galerie Vivienne,
75002 Paris
Tel.: 01 42 60 46 85
Famous for its geometrically-patterned carpets, Casa Lopez also offers embroidery kits on the theme of roses (see page 114).

Sofie Debiève
7, rue Fleuriau,
17000 La Rochelle
Tel.: 05 46 41 07 84
This artist creates works of art exclusively based around dried rose petals (see page 83).

Guillet
99, avenue de La Bourdonnai,
75007 Paris
Tel.: 01 45 51 32 98
Artificial flowers made to order, as well as roses imported from China (see page 9).

Légeron
20, rue des Petits-Champs,
75002 Paris
Tel.: 01 42 96 94 89
Fax: 01 40 15 96 03
Magnificent artificial flowers, hard to tell from the real thing (see pages 94, 95, 96, 97, 98).

Porthault
18, avenue Montaigne,
75008 Paris
Tel.: 01 47 20 75 25
18 East 69th St, NY 10021
Tel.: (212) 688-1660
Delicate, refined table linen embroidered with roses (see pages 102, 110).

Prelle
5, place des Victoires,
75001 Paris
Tel.: 01 42 36 67 21
Founded in Lyons in the eighteenth century, this great name in luxury *à la française* specializes in hand-made,

hand-embroidered fabrics, velvets etc. (see pages 108, 109).

Le Rideau de Paris
32, rue du Bac, 75007 Paris
Tel.: 01 42 61 18 56
A vast range of fabrics, wallpapers, household linen and decorative objects. Florence Maeght, superb designer, will be your guide (see pages 86, 88, 89, 90).

Emilio Robba
63, rue du Bac, 75007 Paris
Tel.: 01 42 60 43 46
There is an unutterable charm to the artificial flowers created by this talented designer (see page 93).

Rose Marie Shulz
30, rue Boissy d'Anglas,
75008 Paris
Tel.: 01 40 17 06 61
Poetry and delicacy are the watchwords of this inspired florist (see page 83).

Trousselier
73, boulevard Haussmann,
75008 Paris
Tel.: 01 42 66 16 16
www.trousselier.com
This store offers you a unique range of sumptuous artificial flowers (see page 101).

United States

Meadows Direct
13805 Highway 136,
Onslow, IA 53231
Tel.: (319) 485-2723
Dried roses for flower arranging enthusiasts.

Tudor Hill Designs
P.O. Box 1405,
South Fallsburg, NY 12779
Tel.: (877) 434-2135
Email: info@tudorhill.com
Fine silk flowers made to order.

Great Britain

Colefax and Fowler
39 Brook Street, London W1 2JE
Tel.: (0207) 493 2231
The best of traditional British fabric design.

Decorative Fabrics Gallery
278-280, Brompton Road,
London SW3 2AS
www.decorativefabrics.co.uk
A huge variety of fabrics on a rose
theme for you to choose from.

Laura Ashley
256–258, Regent Street,
London W1 5DA
Tel.: (0207) 437 9760
www.lauraashley.com

Liberty
214, Regent Street,
London WW1R 6AH
Tel.: (0207) 734 1234
www.liberty.co.uk

TABLEWARE

*Where to find tableware decorated with a
thousand and one roses, whether for
breakfast, afternoon tea, or a formal
evening meal.*

Boutique du Musée
des Arts Décoratifs (see page 91)
105, rue de Rivoli, 75001 Paris
Tel.: 01 42 96 21 31
Didier Gardillou's gorgeous
porcelain roses are available here.

Despalles (see page 112)
26, rue Boissy d'Anglas,
75008 Paris
Tel.: 01 49 24 05 65

Marc Blackwell
134 W. 26th Street,
New York, NY 10001
Tel.: (212) 627-4486
www.marcblackwell.com
Superb hand-painted porcelain.

Monogrammed Linen Shop
168, Walton Street,
London SW3 2JL
Tel.: (0207) 589 4033
Distributor of Porthault's
gorgeous delicate embroidered
table linen.

FASHION

*Fashion and roses have always gone
together. In the following stores you will
find roses flowering in the most
unexpected places...*

Christian Dior
11, rue François 1er, 75008 Paris
Tel.: 01 40 73 54 44
www.dior.com
In particular for the beautifully
delicate silk scarves.

Max Chaoul (see page 103)
55, quai des Grands-Augustins,
75005 Paris
Tel.: 01 43 25 44 02
For summer dresses, with roses to
the fore.

Philippe Model (see page 103)
33, place du Marché Saint-Honoré,
75001 Paris
Tel.: 01 42 96 89 02
Fax: 01 40 20 05 11
Fabulous flowery hats.

Sabbia Rosa (see page 102)
71-73, rue des Saints-Pères,
75006 Paris
Tel.: 01 45 48 88 37
An irresistible choice of lingerie,
with the rose as star of the show.

Agent Provocateur
16, Pont Street
London SW1X 9EN
Tel.: (0207) 235 0229
www.agentprovocateur.com
For gorgeous lingerie.

PERFUMES

*Where to find the exclusive fragrances
cited by the author. But don't forget a
broad range of fine perfumes are
available in major department stores.*

France

Au Nom de la Rose (see page 122)
46, rue du Bac, 75007 Paris
Tel.: 01 42 22 22 12
www.aunomdelarose.fr

Annick Goutal (see page 128)
14, rue de Castiglione, 75001 Paris
Tel.: 01 42 60 52 82

L'Artisan Parfumeur (see page 128)
24, boulevard Raspail, 75007 Paris
Tel.: 01 42 22 23 32

Rose-scented perfumes

For the true rose-lover, here is a
list of perfumes inspired by the
flower's delicate scent:
Joy by Patou,
Paris and Baby Doll by Yves
Saint Laurent,
Or et Noir and Fête des Roses by
Caron,
Nahéma by Guerlain,
China Rose by Floris,
Evelyn by Crabtree and Evelyn,
Abraham Darby by S. and O.
Chantecaille,
A Rose is a Rose by Houbigant,
Rose Absolue by Annick Goutal,
Rykiel Rose by Sonia Rykiel,
Voleur de Roses and Drôle de
Rose by l'Artisan Parfumeur,
Rose Opulente by J.F. Laporte,
Rose de Nuit and Sa Majesté la
Rose by Serge Lutens,
Jardin Secret, Rose Pivoine and
Féerie Rose by Patricia de Nicolaï,
Poiray by Poiray
Trésor, Envol and 2000 et Une
Roses by Lancôme,
not forgetting
l'Heure Bleue by Guerlain,
Calèche by Hermès,
Femme by Rochas,
Shocking by Schiaparelli
and Ombre dans l'Eau by
Diptyque.

Côté Bastide (see page 133)
30, rue Frédéric Joliot,
13000 Aix-en-Provence
Tel.: 04 92 97 31 00

Fragonard (see pages 121, 133)
196, boulevard Saint-Germain,
75007 Paris
Tel.: 01 42 56 06 99
www.fragonard.com

Guerlain (see page 132)
68, Champs-Elysées, 75008 Paris
Tel.: 01 45 62 52 57
www.guerlain.com

Lancôme
29, rue du Faubourg Saint-Honoré,
75008 Paris
Tel.: 01 42 65 30 74
www.lancome.com

L'Occitane (see pages 133,134)
ZI Saint-Maurice, B.P. 307,
04103 Manosque cedex
Tel.: 04 92 70 19 00
www.loccitane.com

Poiray (see page 130)
4, rue de la Paix, 75001 Paris
Tel.: 01 42 97 99 00

Patricia de Nicolaï (see page 130)
69, avenue Poincaré, 75016 Paris
Tel.: 01 47 55 90 92

Sonia Rykiel
175, boulevard Saint-Germain,
75006 Paris
Tel.: 01 49 54 60 60
www.soniarykiel.fr

Yves Saint Laurent Parfums
28, boulevard du Parc,
92200 Neuilly-sur-Seine

United States

Chantecaille (see page 128)
265 Old Chester Road,
Chester, NJ 07930
www.neimanmarcus.com

Great Britain

Crabtree and Evelyn
(see page 128)

38, Neal Street,
Covent Garden, London
Tel.: (0207)240 4963
www.crabtree-evelyn.com

Floris (see page 128)
89 Jermyn Street,
London SW1Y 6JH
Tel.: (0207) 930 2885
www.florislondon.com

Shiseido (see page 129)
Gillingham House,
Gillingham Street,
London SW1V 1HU
Tel.: (0207) 630 1515
www.shiseido.co.uk
www.shiseido.com

FOOD AND DRINK

*The best addresses to enjoy the most
delicious rose-based specialties from
around the world.*

France

Amin Kader (see page 149)
2, rue Guisarde, 75006 Paris
Tel.: 01 43 26 27 37
For the sublime rose elixir from
the Officina di Santa Maria
Novella di Firenze.

Christine Ferber (see page 142)
18, rue des Trois Epis,
68230 Niedermorschwihr
Tel.: 03 89 27 05 69
A huge range of jams and jellies,

including rose-based recipes.
Ladurée (see pages 142, 146)
16, rue Royale, 75008 Paris
Tel.: 01 42 60 21 79
www.laduree.fr
Exquisite rose-flavoured
macaroons.

Goumanyat (see pages 140, 143)
7, rue de la Michodière,
75002 Paris
Tel.: 01 42 68 09 71
Rose liqueurs, comfits, and
cristallized petals.

United States

American Spoon Foods
1668, Clarion Ave., P.O. Box 566,
Petoskey, MI 49770-0566
www.spoon.com
Rose jams and jellies and
fantastic fruit butters.

Great Britain

Whittard of Chelsea
Union Court, 22 Union Road,
London SW4 6JQ
Tel.: (0207) 819 6510
www.whittard.com
Sweetly scented rose-petal tea.

Fortnum and Mason
181 Picadilly, London W1A 1ER
Tel.: (0207) 734 8040
www.fortnumandmason.com
Delicious rose-petal jams,
rosewater, rose essence, and
melt-in-the-mouth Turkish
delight.

SELECTED BIBLIOGRAPHY

Austin, David. *David Austin's English Roses.* Boston: Little, Brown and Company, 1993.
Beales, Peter. *Classic Roses.* New York: Henry Holt and Co., 1985.
Buist, Robert. *The Rose Manual.* 1844. Reprint. New York: Earl M. Coleman, 1978.
Druitt, Liz. *The Organic Rose Garden.* Dallas: Taylor Publishing Co., 1996.
Gibson, Michael, and Donald Myall. *The Book of the Rose.* London: MacDonald General Books, 1980.

Griffiths, Trevor. *The Book of Old Roses.* London: Michael Joseph, 1983.
Jekyll, Gertrude, and Edward Mawley. *Roses for English Gardens.* 1902 Reprint. Woodbridge, UK: Antique Collector's Club, 1982.
Krüssmann, Gerd. *The Complete Book of Roses.* Portland, Oregon: Timber Press, 1981.
Le Rougetel, Hazel. *A Heritage of Old Roses.* London: Unwin Hyman, 1988.
Macoboy, Stirling. *The Ultimate Rose Book.* New York: Harry N.

Abrams, Inc., 1993.
Moody, Mary, and Peter Harkness, Eds. *The Illustrated Encyclopedia of Roses.* Portland, Oregon: Timber Press, 1992.
Ohrbach, Barbara. *Roses for the Scented Room.* New York: Clarkson Potter, 2000.
Park, Bertram. *Collins Guide to Roses.* London: Collins, 1969.
Phillips, Rodger, and Martyn Rix. *The Random House Guide to Roses.* New York: Random House, 1988.
Reddell, Rayford C. *The Rose Bible.* New York: Harmony Press, 1994.

PHOTOGRAPHIC CREDITS

All photographs featured in this book are the work of Christian Sarramon, except:
p. 7: Stair Santy Gallery, New York; p. 8: D.R.; p. 9: top, Deidi von Schaewen, bottom, Harkness & Co; p 10: D. Michalet/Private collection; p. 11: RMN-Arnaudet; p. 12: Bridgeman-Giraudon; p. 13: top, the Bridgeman Art Library, bottom, Bridgeman-Giraudon; p.14: top, the Bridgeman Art Library, Whitford & Hugues, London; p. 15: D.R.; p.16: top, the Fine Art Photographic Library, bottom, Pierre Ferbos/Studio Flammarion; p. 19: Vincent Motte; p. 22/23: Deidi von Schaewen; p. 26: top, Elizabeth Bourgeois; p. 28: Vincent Motte; p. 29: bottom, Vincent Motte; p. 30: top and bottom, Deidi von Schaewen; p. 32/33: Vincent Motte; p. 34: top and bottom, Vincent Motte; p. 38: top, Vincent Motte; p. 42: top and bottom, Deidi von Schaewen; p. 43: Vincent Motte; p. 45: Vincent Motte; p. 47: P. Ferret (*ABCdaire des roses*); p. 48: Catalogue David Austin; p. 51: top, Deidi von Schaewen; p. 52: Deidi von Schaewen; p. 55: Marc Walter; p. 57: top, Marc Walter; p. 58/59: Marc Walter; p. 60: top, Alte Pinakothek, Munich-The Bridgeman Art Library, bottom, Marc Walter/coll. M. and Mme Kenber; p. 61: Patrick Jacob/Agence Top; p. 76: Christophe Dugied; p. 84/85: Marc Walter; p. 98/99: Marc Walter; p.102: bottom, J. Boulay; p.104: bottom, Musée de Mulhouse/David Soyer; p. 105/106/107: Mauny wallpapers; p. 110: top and bottom, J. Boulay; p. 11: Jean-Pierre Dieterlen; p. 113: V&A Picture Library; p. 117: Christopher Wood Gallery, London; p. 118: J. Boulay; p. 119: Ali von Bothmer; p. 120: Cyril le Tourneur d'Ison/Chanel; p. 121: SIP/Côté Sud/N. Mackenzie; p. 122/123: Fragonard; p. 124: Cécile Tréal/Jean-Michel Ruiz; p. 125: top, Cornucopia, bottom, Givaudan-Roure; p.126: top, Fragonard; p. 142: bottom, Pierre Ferbos/Studio Flammarion; p. 143: Jérôme Darblay; p. 144: top, Pierre Ferbos/Studio Flammarion; p. 150: top, Pierre Ferbos/Studio Flammarion, bottom, Jean-Charles Vaillant; p. 151: Magazine Victoria, New York

ACKNOWLEDGEMENTS

The author wishes to thank Ghislaine Bavoillot for the chance to write about such a fascinating subject, as well as all the Art de Vivre editing team, in particular Maud Hannon, Nathalie Labrousse, Anne Bouvier, and Hélène Boulanger.

The photographer wishes to express his gratitude for the co-operation of the following stores: Michèle Aragon, Conran Shop, Designers Guild, La Grande Epicerie du Bon Marché, Habitat, Il pour l'homme, Israël, Taïr Mercier, Marie Papier.

Special thanks go to: Jean-Luc Averland, Martin Dimier, Lise Fournier, Inès Sarramon, Charlotte Sauvat.

The editor wishes to thank all the stores, designers, perfumers, and creators who so kindly contributed the material necessary for the creation of this book:

Agnès B., L'Artisan Parfumeur, Bernardaud, Elsa C., Caron, Casa Lopez, Chantecaille, Max Chaoul, Colefax and Fowler, Compagnie Française de l'Orient et de la Chine, Côté Bastide, Sofie Debiève, Despalles, Dior, Dyptique, Entrée des Fournisseurs, Espace Rugby, Au Fil des Couleurs, Floris, Les Folies d'Elodie, Fouquet, Fragonard, Goumanyat, Annick Goutal, Guerlain, Amin Kader, Christian Lacroix, Ladurée, Lancôme, Jean-François Laporte, Philippe Model, Moschino, Boutique du Musée des Arts Décoratifs, Patricia de Nicolaï, Noël, L'Occitane, Patou, Poiray, Porthault, Prelle, Raynaud, Résonnances, Le Rideau de Paris, Emilio Robba, Roger et Gallet, Sonia Rykiel, Sabbia Rosa, Yves Saint Laurent, Rose-Marie Schulz, Shiseïdo.

Very warm thanks also to the florists who created bouquets especially for this book and who taught us so much about the rose and its style: Au Nom de la Rose, Baptiste, Stéphane Chapelle, Comme à la Campagne, Comme une Fleur, Céline Dussaule, Un Fleuriste, Georges François, Les Mille Feuilles, Moulié, Christian Tortu.

The editor also wishes to thank Mme. Samantha Adam, journalist for *Figaro Madame* magazine, M. Jean-Luc Blais, designer of Claudia Cardinale's dining room, Mme. Anne-Laure Legrand, who helped us with our research at Prelle, Mme. Florence Maeght of Le Rideau de Paris, M. Magnan of Casa Lopez, M. Mauny for his precious help concerning wallpapers, and Mme. Texier of Au Fil des Couleurs.

Finally, the editor also wishes to extend most sincere thanks to Sylvie Girard, Christian Sarramon, Vincent Motte, Valérie Gautier, Maud Hannon, and Sylvie Creuze, who have shared in this rose-scented adventure with enthusiasm.